MY FINAL ANSWER

2 Complete Faith-Based Trivia Challenges

BARBOUR
PUBLISHING

ISBN 978-1-60260-793-4

Published by Barbour Publishing, Inc., P. O. Box 719, Uhrichsville, Ohio 44683, www.barbourbooks.com

Our mission is to publish and distribute inspirational products offering exceptional value and biblical encouragement to the masses.

ecpa Member of the Evangelical Christian Publishers Association

Printed in the United States of America.

INTRODUCTION

Here's the trivia book you've been waiting for!

Each of the 60 quizzes in this book—30 Bible trivia quizzes and 30 quizzes on Christian history—will test your knowledge with fun, interesting, and increasingly more difficult questions. Read My Final Answer for yourself, or use it in a group—the book's setup lends itself well to a "quiz show" format, with a contestant and a moderator.

Each quiz features twelve levels of multiple-choice questions, beginning with easy material you might have learned in your Sunday school years. But the challenge increases as you move through the levels. Get through four levels without a wrong answer, and you'll earn a (figurative) Bronze Medal. If you can successfully navigate eight levels of questions, you'll win Silver. And if you can complete all twelve levels without a miss, you'll take the Gold!

Be forewarned, though—you'll need to know your Bible and Christian history very well to answer those higher level questions.

But you will have help. In each quiz, you get three Bonuses. Use them carefully, in conjunction with your knowledge, and you can win! Once in each quiz you can:

Double Your Chances: Look up this bonus to learn two of the wrong answers.

Have a Hint: Look up this Bonus to get some extra information—it may be a word play or some reference to the popular culture—to give you a clue to the correct answer.

Look in the Book: Look up this Bonus for a Bible reference to review. . .then find your final answer in the final authority.

Remember: You get a total of three Bonuses (one of each) in each twelve-question quiz. And please note that all Bonuses, like the answers, are listed by level rather than by quiz. That way, you won't inadvertently see information on the next question as you're checking out your current one.

Answers for *My Final Answer* begin on page 183.
Answers for *My Final Answer—Celebrity Edition* start on page 373.

One final note: Direct Bible quotations in the questions are taken from the New International Version of the Bible—but they should be general enough for those more familiar with other scripture translations.

So are you ready for the challenge? Step up to the "hot seat" and show us your knowledge. As you prove how much you know, keep in mind James 1:22—about the importance of *acting* on what you know. That's what the knowledge of the faith is all about—and that's *My Final Answer*!

MY FINAL ANSWER

BIBLE TRIVIA

THIRTY INTERACTIVE QUIZZES
THAT PUT *YOU* IN THE HOT SEAT

PAUL KENT

Quizzes

BIBLE TRIVIA

THIRTY INTERACTIVE QUIZZES THAT PUT YOU IN THE HOT SEAT

QUIZ 1

LEVEL 1

What was the name of the first man?

a) Fred
b) Adam
c) Noah
d) John the Baptist

LEVEL 2

Which disciple betrayed Jesus for thirty pieces of silver?

a) Andrew
b) Simon the Zealot
c) Judas Iscariot
d) Philip

Pages 147–148 Pages 159–160 Pages 171–172 Pages 183–184

Level 3

What personal friend did Jesus raise from the dead?

a) Lazarus
b) John
c) Mary
d) Martha

Bronze

According to the apostle Paul, the wages of sin is what?

a) disease
b) pain
c) death
d) grief

Level 5

With what woman did King David commit adultery?

a) Bathsheba
b) Hannah
c) Delilah
d) Tamar

Level 6

Isaiah prophesied that Jesus would be "a man of" what?

a) joy
b) sorrows
c) power
d) pain

Pages 149–152 Pages 161–164 Pages 173–176 Pages 185–188

Level 7

According to the apostle Paul, what "governmental" role do believers play for Christ?

a) tax collectors
b) governors
c) ambassadors
d) commissioners

Silver

According to David, how far has God "removed our transgressions from us"?

a) as far as the east is from the west
b) as far as the earth is from the stars
c) as far as a man can travel
d) as far as the light can pierce the darkness

Level 9

In the book of John, Jesus said the world would recognize His disciples by what?

a) their faith
b) their good works
c) their love
d) their wisdom

Pages 153–155 Pages 165–167 Pages 177–179 Pages 189–191

Level 10

To whom is the book of Acts addressed?

a) Theophilus
b) Barnabas
c) Cornelius
d) Eutychus

Level 11

Where did Moses flee after killing an Egyptian?

a) Mesopotamia
b) Megiddo
c) Mitylene
d) Midian

Gold

What Old Testament prophet was a shepherd from Tekoa?

a) Micah
b) Nahum
c) Amos
d) Zechariah

Pages 156–158 Pages 168–170 Pages 180–182 Pages 192–194

QUIZ 2

LEVEL 1

Who built an ark to protect his family, seven of every clean animal, and two of every unclean animal from a devastating worldwide flood?

a) Moses
b) Abraham
c) Noah
d) Captain Kangaroo

LEVEL 2

How does John 3:16 begin?

a) "In the beginning God..."
b) "But those who hope in the Lord..."
c) "But God demonstrates his own love..."
d) "For God so loved the world..."

Pages 147–148 Pages 159–160 Pages 171–172 Pages 183–184

Level 3

What baby, a future Israelite leader, was placed in a basket in the Nile River?

a) Joseph
b) Moses
c) David
d) Nehemiah

Bronze

What Roman governor allowed the crucifixion of Jesus?

a) Quirinius
b) Pilate
c) Felix
d) Festus

Level 5

According to the apostle Paul, how will the day of Jesus' return come?

a) like a thief in the night
b) like a mighty trumpet
c) like a flash of lightning
d) like an eagle swooping

Pages 149–151 Pages 161–163 Pages 173–175 Pages 185–187

LEVEL 6

Who was Jacob's father?

a) Abraham
b) Lot
c) Isaac
d) Joseph

LEVEL 7

Which of the following is *not* on the apostle Paul's list of things to think about?

a) whatever is true
b) whatever is pure
c) whatever is lovely
d) whatever is pleasing

SILVER

What king's prayer added fifteen years to his life?

a) David
b) Hezekiah
c) Jehoshaphat
d) Ahaziah

LEVEL 9

After the crucifixion, who asked Pilate for Jesus' body?

a) Simon of Cyrene
b) Joseph of Arimathea
c) Mary of Magdala
d) Apollos of Alexandria

Pages 152–155 Pages 164–167 Pages 176–179 Pages 188–191

Level 10

Which of the following is *not* listed as part of King Nebuchadnezzar's punishment for pride?

a) He ate grass like cattle.
b) His hair grew like a bird's feathers.
c) His nails grew like a bird's claws.
d) He slept in a wet cave.

Level 11

What king died in the year that Isaiah received his commission from the Lord?

a) Amaziah
b) Uzziah
c) Jotham
d) Ahaz

Gold

Which of these churches of Asia Minor did Jesus threaten to spit from His mouth?

a) Ephesus
b) Smyrna
c) Philadelphia
d) Laodicea

Pages 156–158 Pages 168–170 Pages 180–182 Pages 192–194

BIBLE TRIVIA

THIRTY INTERACTIVE QUIZZES THAT PUT YOU IN THE HOT SEAT

QUIZ 3

LEVEL 1

Who conquered the warrior Goliath?

a) David
b) Jonathan
c) Malachi
d) Jack the Giant Killer

LEVEL 2

What judge of Israel was known for his long hair and great strength?

a) Tola
b) Samson
c) Gideon
d) Hercules

Pages 147–148 Pages 159–160 Pages 171–172 Pages 183–184

Level 3

Who cursed the day of his birth after suffering multiple attacks of Satan?

a) Jacob
b) Ezekiel
c) Job
d) Malachi

Bronze

Who wrote the book of Revelation?

a) John
b) James
c) Jude
d) Jeremiah

Level 5

According to Jesus, it is less likely for a rich man to enter God's kingdom than for a camel to what?

a) fly
b) go through the eye of a needle
c) speak
d) have triplets

Level 6

According to the book of 1 Timothy, what is a "root of all kinds of evil"?

a) pride
b) sex
c) Satan
d) the love of money

Pages 149–152 Pages 161–164 Pages 173–176 Pages 185–188

Level 7

On which mountain did Noah's ark settle as the great flood subsided?

a) Ararat
b) Hermon
c) Moriah
d) Nebo

Silver

Which of the following was *not* one of Satan's temptations of Christ?

a) changing stones into bread
b) jumping off the temple
c) worshiping the devil
d) striking the wicked with blindness

Level 9

"Golgotha," the site of Jesus' crucifixion, means what?

a) the Hill of Sorrows
b) the Potter's Field
c) the Place of the Skull
d) the Well of the Oath

Pages 153–155 Pages 165–167 Pages 177–179 Pages 189–191

LEVEL 10

Who deserted Paul and Barnabas, and their missionary work, in Pamphylia?

a) Silas
b) John Mark
c) Judas Barsabbas
d) Linus

LEVEL 11

Which of the following is *not* a part of the famous "a time for everything" passage in Ecclesiastes?

a) a time to be born and a time to die
b) a time to sleep and a time to wake
c) a time to weep and a time to laugh
d) a time to love and a time to hate

GOLD

What was the name of the man who had an ear cut off, and healed, during Christ's arrest?

a) Malchus
b) Zenas
c) Aristarchus
d) Archippus

Pages 156–158 Pages 168–170 Pages 180–182 Pages 192–194

QUIZ 4

LEVEL 1

What was the name of Jesus' mother?

a) Ruth
b) Esther
c) Martha
d) Mary

LEVEL 2

How does the famous 23rd Psalm begin?

a) "The earth is the Lord's..."
b) "The Lord is my shepherd..."
c) "Blessed is the man..."
d) "Great is the Lord..."

Pages 147–148 Pages 159–160 Pages 171–172 Pages 183–184

LEVEL 3

Before his conversion, what was the apostle Paul's name?

a) Simon
b) Elymas
c) Saul
d) Moses

BRONZE

Who committed the first murder?

a) Adam
b) Cain
c) Abel
d) Lamech

LEVEL 5

Which disciple demanded to see the nail prints in Jesus' hands and feet before he would believe in the Resurrection?

a) Bartholomew
b) James
c) Simon the Zealot
d) Thomas

LEVEL 6

According to the apostle Paul, what kind of giver does God love?

a) cheerful
b) generous
c) prompt
d) regular

Pages 149–152 Pages 161–164 Pages 173–176 Pages 185–188

Level 7

Which of the following is *not* among the names of Christ in Isaiah's prophecy?

a) Mighty God
b) Everlasting Father
c) Prince of Peace
d) Hope of Man

Silver

What woman, known for her good works, did Peter raise from the dead in Joppa?

a) Tabitha
b) Lydia
c) Drusilla
d) Bernice

Level 9

Which of the following did *not* appear at the Transfiguration?

a) Jesus
b) Moses
c) Elijah
d) Samuel

Pages 153–155 Pages 165–167 Pages 177–179 Pages 189–191

Level 10

Who helped carry Jesus' cross to Golgotha?

a) Micah of Moresheth
b) Simon of Cyrene
c) Joseph of Arimathea
d) Joseph of Cyprus

Level 11

Who died after touching the Ark of the Covenant?

a) Uzzah
b) Mahlon
c) Ahio
d) Naphtali

Gold

Sanballat and Tobiah are villains in what biblical book?

a) Esther
b) Nehemiah
c) Obadiah
d) Daniel

Pages 156–158 Pages 168–170 Pages 180–182 Pages 192–194

THIRTY INTERACTIVE QUIZZES THAT PUT YOU IN THE HOT SEAT

BIBLE TRIVIA

QUIZ 5

LEVEL 1

What set of rules did God give to Moses?

a) the Four Spiritual Laws
b) the Seven Habits of Highly Successful People
c) the Ten Commandments
d) the Twelve-Step Program

Page 147 Page 159 Page 171 Page 183

Level 2

According to the book of Revelation, the streets of the New Jerusalem are made of what?

a) gold
b) silver
c) cedar
d) asphalt

Level 3

According to Psalm 119, God's Word is a lamp to what?

a) my feet
b) the darkness
c) His people
d) the blind

Bronze

What did the apostle Paul call the ninefold characteristics (love, joy, peace, etc.) of the maturing Christian?

a) the harvest of faith
b) the works of the righteous
c) the fruit of the Spirit
d) the life of Christ

Pages 148–150 Pages 160–162 Pages 172–174 Pages 184–186

Level 5

How did Judas Iscariot kill himself after betraying Jesus?

a) by hanging
b) by drinking poison
c) by jumping off a cliff
d) by drowning

Level 6

Who had a donkey that spoke?

a) Ahab
b) Jehoshaphat
c) Solomon
d) Balaam

Level 7

What is the more commonly known name of the Bible character Hadassah?

a) Abraham
b) Esther
c) Gideon
d) Mary Magdalene

Pages 151–153 Pages 163–165 Pages 175–177 Pages 187–189

Silver

According to the apostle Paul, what never fails?

a) love
b) truth
c) faith
d) God

Level 9

According to the book of Hebrews, Jesus is a high priest in the order of whom?

a) Aaron
b) Joshua
c) Eleazar
d) Melchizedek

Level 10

Who was known as a "mighty hunter before the Lord"?

a) David
b) Gideon
c) Nimrod
d) Ishmael

Pages 154–156 Pages 166–168 Pages 178–180 Pages 190–192

Level 11

What was the name of the servant girl who met Peter after an angel freed him from prison?

a) Lydia
b) Euodia
c) Rhoda
d) Priscilla

Gold

Which of the following is *not* a physical compliment from the Song of Solomon?

a) "Your nose is like the tower of Lebanon."
b) "Your navel is a rounded goblet."
c) "Your fingers are like limbs of cedar."
d) "Your eyes are the pools of Heshbon."

Pages 157–158 Pages 169–170 Pages 181–182 Pages 193–194

Quiz 6

Level 1

What did Adam name his wife?

a) Eve
b) Sarah
c) Rachel
d) Honey

Level 2

What was the vocation of Jesus' earthly father, Joseph?

a) priest
b) shepherd
c) carpenter
d) farmer

Pages 147–148 Pages 159–160 Pages 171–172 Pages 183–184

LEVEL 3

Which of the following is *not* one of the Ten Commandments?

a) You shall not murder.
b) You shall not steal.
c) Honor your father and mother.
d) You shall not gossip.

BRONZE

Which of the following is *not* a "fruit of the Spirit"?

a) love
b) health
c) peace
d) goodness

LEVEL 5

What was the apostle Paul's hometown?

a) Jerusalem
b) Joppa
c) Tarsus
d) Antioch

LEVEL 6

According to Jesus, "the greatest among you will be. . ."

a) "the winner of souls."
b) "the worker of miracles."
c) "your teacher."
d) "your servant."

Pages 149–152 Pages 161–164 Pages 173–176 Pages 185–188

Level 7

What man was struck dead for lying about the amount of money he gave to God?

a) Silas
b) Bartimaeus
c) Ananias
d) Nicolas

Silver

What group of people was commended for comparing Paul's teachings with the scriptures?

a) the Thessalonians
b) the Bereans
c) the Colossians
d) the Galatians

Level 9

In a vision of Isaiah, what were the seraphs over the Lord's throne calling one to another?

a) "Holy, holy, holy"
b) "The Lord God omnipotent reigneth"
c) "Glory to God in the highest"
d) "Praise the Lord"

Pages 153–155 Pages 165–167 Pages 177–179 Pages 189–191

Level 10

What character in the story of Esther was hanged on a gallows that he had ordered built?

a) Mordecai
b) Xerxes
c) Haman
d) Harbona

Level 11

Which of the following is *not* listed as a source for the book of Proverbs?

a) Job
b) Solomon
c) King Lemuel
d) Agur

Gold

Who wrote down the book of Romans for the apostle Paul?

a) Lucius
b) Jason
c) Tertius
d) Erastus

Pages 156–158 Pages 168–170 Pages 180–182 Pages 192–194

THIRTY INTERACTIVE QUIZZES THAT PUT YOU IN THE HOT SEAT

BIBLE TRIVIA

QUIZ 7

LEVEL 1

What prophet spent three nights in a fish's stomach?

a) Obadiah
b) Joel
c) Jonah
d) Micah

LEVEL 2

According to the psalmist, God owns what on a thousand hills?

a) the cellular phone towers
b) the cattle
c) the dwellings
d) the oak trees

Pages 147–148 Pages 159–160 Pages 171–172 Pages 183–184

Level 3

From what miraculous thing did Moses receive his call to leadership?

a) a staff that became a snake
b) a burning bush
c) a rock that gushed forth water
d) a healed leper

Bronze

Which of the following was *not* a son of Noah?

a) Ham
b) Japheth
c) Kenan
d) Shem

Level 5

In what town did Jesus spend His youth?

a) Jerusalem
b) Nazareth
c) Bethlehem
d) Tyre

Level 6

What prophet was taken to heaven in a whirlwind?

a) Elijah
b) Obadiah
c) Samuel
d) Zephaniah

Pages 149–152 Pages 161–164 Pages 173–176 Pages 185–188

LEVEL 7

What kept Paul from becoming conceited over his special vision of heaven?

a) a thorn in the flesh
b) his partnership with Timothy
c) the deacons of the church of Corinth
d) his discipline of service

SILVER

What title did God tell Moses to use when answering the Israelites' question, "What is his [God's] name?"

a) Jehovah
b) Yahweh
c) I AM
d) The Lord of Hosts

LEVEL 9

Whom did Eve say "replaced" the murdered Abel?

a) Seth
b) Enosh
c) Jared
d) Lamech

Pages 153–155 Pages 165–167 Pages 177–179 Pages 189–191

Level 10

What was the apostle Paul's rule toward people who refused to work?

a) They should be prayed over.
b) They should not eat.
c) They should be disciplined by the church.
d) They should not expect charity.

Level 11

How many siblings, the natural children of Mary and Joseph, did Jesus have?

a) none
b) two
c) four
d) six or more

Gold

According to the Proverbs, what is true of an adulterous woman's speech?

a) It is smoother than oil.
b) It has ensnared many young men.
c) It is full of lies.
d) It can confuse the wise.

Pages 156–158 Pages 168–170 Pages 180–182 Pages 192–194

QUIZ 8

LEVEL 1

What new name did God give Abram?

a) Abraham
b) Abel
c) Adam
d) Apple of My Eye

LEVEL 2

Which disciple disowned Jesus three times the night of Christ's arrest?

a) Andrew
b) James
c) Philip
d) Peter

Pages 147–148 Pages 159–160 Pages 171–172 Pages 183–184

Level 3

What was the name of Moses' brother?

a) Abraham
b) Zipporah
c) Aaron
d) Zebulun

Bronze

Where does God keep a record of the names of the saved?

a) the book of heaven
b) the book of life
c) the book of the blessed
d) the book of the kingdom

Level 5

According to Jesus, what belongs to the "poor in spirit"?

a) the joy of the Lord
b) the kingdom of heaven
c) the water of life
d) the wisdom of Solomon

Pages 149–151 Pages 161–163 Pages 173–175 Pages 185–187

LEVEL 6

Of the twelve men who spied in Canaan, how many believed the Israelites should go in to possess the land?

a) twelve
b) eight
c) two
d) none

LEVEL 7

Who "walked with God; then he was no more, because God took him away"?

a) Methuselah
b) Enoch
c) Benjamin
d) Caleb

SILVER

What miraculous thing did Elisha make an axe head do?

a) speak
b) turn to gold
c) float
d) heal lepers

Pages 152–154 Pages 164–166 Pages 176–178 Pages 188–190

Level 9

What did some mockers say of the disciples who spoke in other tongues during Pentecost?

a) "They are possessed by devils."
b) "They are only pretending."
c) "They have had too much wine."
d) "They have lost their minds."

Level 10

What miraculous event accompanied Joshua's military victory over the Amorites?

a) His dead soldiers returned to life.
b) The earth swallowed his enemies.
c) An angel struck his opponents blind.
d) The sun stood still for a day.

Level 11

Job was from the land of what?

a) Uz
b) On
c) Ur
d) Og

Gold

Which of the following groups of stars is mentioned in scripture?

a) Gemini
b) Pleiades
c) Perseus
d) Cassiopeia

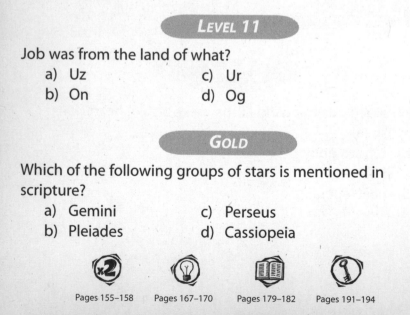

Pages 155–158 Pages 167–170 Pages 179–182 Pages 191–194

THIRTY INTERACTIVE QUIZZES THAT PUT YOU IN THE HOT SEAT

BIBLE TRIVIA

QUIZ 9

LEVEL 1

Which of the following was not one of Jesus' original disciples?

a) Peter
b) John
c) Moses
d) Matthew

LEVEL 2

What was Adam and Eve's original home?

a) the Garden of Eden
b) the Plains of Moab
c) the Valley of Jericho
d) the Big Apple

Pages 147–148 Pages 159–160 Pages 171–172 Pages 183–184

LEVEL 3

What man in David's life "loved him as himself"?

a) Saul
b) Joab
c) Abner
d) Jonathan

BRONZE

Where did God confuse the language of the early humans?

a) Babel
b) Sodom
c) Gomorrah
d) Nineveh

LEVEL 5

According to the psalmist, what do the heavens declare?

a) the glory of God
b) the wonders of creation
c) the beauty of holiness
d) the strength of the Lord

LEVEL 6

What symbolic action did Pontius Pilate take to argue his own innocence in the crucifixion of Jesus?

a) He put on a blindfold.
b) He turned his back on the crowd.
c) He released a dove.
d) He washed his hands.

Pages 149–152 Pages 161–164 Pages 173–176 Pages 185–188

Level 7

The apostle Paul warned Christians about being "yoked" with what?

a) debt
b) unbelievers
c) sin
d) worldly wisdom

Silver

What was the nationality of the giant warrior Goliath?

a) Philistine
b) Moabite
c) Phoenician
d) Ammonite

Level 9

Why did Peter rebuke a new convert formerly known as "Simon the sorcerer"?

a) for returning to his sorcery
b) for calling down curses on Pharisees
c) for casting out demons without permission
d) for trying to buy the gift of the Holy Spirit

Pages 153–155 Pages 165–167 Pages 177–179 Pages 189–191

LEVEL 10

What vocation did the apostle Paul have in addition to his missionary work?

a) carpentry
b) fishing
c) tentmaking
d) vinedressing

LEVEL 11

Why did the residents of Malta think the apostle Paul was a god?

a) He raised someone from the dead.
b) A snake bite didn't kill him.
c) He predicted a terrible storm.
d) Angels appeared to strengthen him.

GOLD

What idol fell to the ground and broke after the Ark of the Covenant was placed nearby?

a) Dagon
b) Ashtaroth
c) Molech
d) Chemosh

Pages 156–158 Pages 168–170 Pages 180–182 Pages 192–194

QUIZ 10

LEVEL 1

What punishment did Shadrach, Meschach, and Abednego receive for refusing to worship a golden image?

a) the lions' den
b) the fiery furnace
c) the gallows
d) the bagpipes

LEVEL 2

According to the book of Romans, who has sinned and fallen short of God's glory?

a) Jews
b) Gentiles
c) pagans
d) all

Pages 147–148 Pages 159–160 Pages 171–172 Pages 183–184

LEVEL 3

Jesus said, "I am the vine, you are the" what?

a) grapes
b) leaves
c) branches
d) thorns

BRONZE

Who was specially commissioned as Moses' successor as leader of Israel?

a) Aaron
b) Joshua
c) Eli
d) Nehemiah

LEVEL 5

In the "armor of God," what does the shield represent?

a) salvation
b) righteousness
c) faith
d) truth

LEVEL 6

According to the apostle Paul, how are husbands supposed to love their wives?

a) as Abraham cared for Sarah
b) as Christ loved the church
c) as the Spirit gives them power
d) as the hen protects her chicks

Pages 149–152 Pages 161–164 Pages 173–176 Pages 185–188

LEVEL 7

The "potter's field," purchased with the money Judas Iscariot received for betraying Christ, was also known as what?

a) the Field of Blood
b) the Field of Sorrows
c) the Field of Agony
d) the Betrayer's Field

SILVER

According to the apostle Paul, godliness with what is "great gain"?

a) peace
b) love
c) contentment
d) friendship

LEVEL 9

What Old Testament book was the Ethiopian eunuch reading when Philip led him to Christ?

a) Psalms
b) Proverbs
c) Isaiah
d) Jeremiah

Pages 153–155 Pages 165–167 Pages 177–179 Pages 189–191

Level 10

Which disciple was the first to enter Jesus' empty tomb?

a) John
b) Peter
c) Matthew
d) Thomas

Level 11

As a tribute to Jonathan, what descendant of Saul ate at King David's table?

a) Malki-Shua
b) Melech
c) Micah
d) Mephibosheth

Gold

According to the Proverbs, a prostitute reduces a man to what?

a) a brute beast
b) a blind beggar
c) a blemished bull
d) a bite of bread

Pages 156–158 Pages 168–170 Pages 180–182 Pages 192–194

THIRTY INTERACTIVE QUIZZES THAT PUT YOU IN THE HOT SEAT

BIBLE TRIVIA

Quiz 11

Level 1

What did God do on the seventh day of the creation week?

a) He created man.
b) He created light.
c) He created music.
d) He rested.

Level 2

What sign sealed God's promise never again to destroy the earth by a flood?

a) the rainbow
b) the bronze serpent
c) the pillar of fire
d) the man in the moon

Pages 147–148 Pages 159–160 Pages 171–172 Pages 183–184

Level 3

What did Peter notice immediately after his third denial of Christ—just as Jesus had predicted?

a) a shooting star
b) a mourner's wail
c) a peal of thunder
d) a rooster crowing

Bronze

What special test did God give Abraham?

a) to sacrifice his son Isaac
b) to fast forty days in the desert
c) to kill one thousand Philistines
d) to give all he owned to the poor

Level 5

On which mountain did Moses receive the Ten Commandments?

a) Mount Carmel
b) Mount Nebo
c) Mount Gilboa
d) Mount Sinai

Level 6

What advice did Job's wife have for her suffering husband?

a) "Sacrifice a burnt offering."
b) "Accept your lot from God."
c) "Curse God and die."
d) "Renounce your sin."

Pages 149–152 Pages 161–164 Pages 173–176 Pages 185–188

Level 7

According to the apostle Paul, "it is better to marry than to" what?

a) taste the riches of this world
b) speak in tongues
c) burn with passion
d) serve the Lord alone

Silver

According to James, what can no man tame?

a) the lion
b) the eyes
c) the devil
d) the tongue

Level 9

What was Nehemiah's role in the service of King Artaxerxes?

a) royal historian
b) baker
c) cupbearer
d) military commander

Pages 153–155 Pages 165–167 Pages 177–179 Pages 189–191

Level 10

In which city did Paul preach about the "unknown god" to the local philosophers?

a) Athens
b) Berea
c) Corinth
d) Derbe

Level 11

What is the better-known name of Belteshazzar?

a) Aaron
b) Daniel
c) Ezekiel
d) Moses

Gold

What judge of Israel had thirty sons who rode thirty donkeys?

a) Tola
b) Jair
c) Jephthah
d) Eli

Pages 156–158 Pages 168–170 Pages 180–182 Pages 192–194

QUIZ 12

LEVEL 1

How many apostles did Jesus personally select?

a) two
b) twelve
c) fifty
d) one thousand

LEVEL 2

On what "twin cities" did God rain fire and brimstone?

a) Minneapolis and St. Paul
b) Tyre and Sidon
c) Sodom and Gomorrah
d) Athens and Corinth

Pages 147–148 Pages 159–160 Pages 171–172 Pages 183–184

LEVEL 3

Who tested the Lord's will with a fleece?

a) David
b) Gideon
c) Obadiah
d) Lot

BRONZE

In their very first meeting, what did Jesus say He would make of Peter and Andrew?

a) workers of miracles
b) servants of God
c) teachers of rabbis
d) fishers of men

LEVEL 5

What queen, upon visiting Solomon, raved that "not even half" of his wisdom and achievements had been told to her?

a) the queen of Sheba
b) Queen Esther
c) Queen Jezebel
d) Queen Athaliah

LEVEL 6

According to the Proverbs, what are we not to "lean on"?

a) a crooked staff
b) our own understanding
c) a double-minded man
d) the riches of this world

Pages 149–152 Pages 161–164 Pages 173–176 Pages 185–188

LEVEL 7

What phrase from the book of Genesis describes the marriage of a man and a woman?

a) one flesh
b) holy union
c) children of God
d) great reward

SILVER

According to the Proverbs, a good name is what?

a) better than great riches
b) difficult to maintain
c) the heritage of the Lord's children
d) its own reward

LEVEL 9

Which of David's wives was a daughter of King Saul?

a) Michal
b) Abigail
c) Bathsheba
d) Ahinoam

Pages 153–155 Pages 165–167 Pages 177–179 Pages 189–191

LEVEL 10

What vision convinced Peter to share the gospel with the Gentiles?

a) a man of Macedonia
b) the third heaven
c) animals in a sheet
d) angels on a ladder

LEVEL 11

Who discovered a Jewish plot to kill the apostle Paul?

a) Paul's nephew
b) Timothy
c) Silas
d) Barnabas

GOLD

According to Jude, what did the devil and Michael the archangel fight over?

a) the conversion of Saul
b) the temptation of Jesus
c) the mind of Judas Iscariot
d) the body of Moses

Pages 156–158 Pages 168–170 Pages 180–182 Pages 192–194

BIBLE TRIVIA

THIRTY INTERACTIVE QUIZZES THAT PUT YOU IN THE HOT SEAT

QUIZ 13

LEVEL 1

Who climbed a sycamore tree to see Jesus?

a) Zacchaeus
b) Nicodemus
c) Lazarus
d) Curious George

LEVEL 2

Which of the following rivers was *not* a branch of the river that watered the Garden of Eden?

a) Gihon
b) Tigris
c) Euphrates
d) Danube

Pages 147–148 Pages 159–160 Pages 171–172 Pages 183–184

Level 3

Which of the following was a missionary companion of the apostle Paul?

a) Barnabas
b) Barbados
c) Bar-Jesus
d) Barabbas

Bronze

What is the first of the Ten Commandments?

a) You shall not murder.
b) You shall not commit adultery.
c) You shall have no other gods before me.
d) Honor your father and your mother.

Level 5

What sign protected Israelite homes in Egypt from the plague on the firstborn?

a) a candle in the window
b) bread in the oven
c) a goat in the yard
d) blood on the doorposts

Pages 149–151 Pages 161–163 Pages 173–175 Pages 185–187

Level 6

According to Jesus, what would not fall to the ground apart from God's will?

a) a sparrow
b) a rain drop
c) a leaf
d) brimstone

Level 7

Which biblical man had the longest recorded lifespan?

a) Adam
b) Isaac
c) Methuselah
d) Noah

Silver

Which of the following disciples was *not* with Jesus when He was arrested at Gethsemane?

a) Andrew
b) Peter
c) James
d) John

Level 9

Which tribe was in charge of assembling, disassembling, and moving the tabernacle?

a) the tribe of Reuben
b) the tribe of Dan
c) the tribe of Levi
d) the tribe of Judah

Pages 152–155 Pages 164–167 Pages 176–179 Pages 188–191

Level 10

What destroyed the golden-headed statue in King Nebuchadnezzar's dream?

a) a violent whirlwind
b) a flood of the Euphrates River
c) a mighty angel of God
d) a rock not cut by human hands

Level 11

In what city did followers of the false goddess Artemis (Diana) riot after Paul's preaching?

a) Ephesus
b) Corinth
c) Rome
d) Philippi

Gold

The book of Nahum prophesies the fall of what city?

a) Babylon
b) Tyre
c) Susa
d) Nineveh

Pages 156–158 Pages 168–170 Pages 180–182 Pages 192–194

QUIZ 14

LEVEL 1

What example did Jesus use to define the word "neighbor"?

a) the good American
b) the good Egyptian
c) the good Samaritan
d) the good Philistine

LEVEL 2

What did David use to battle Goliath?

a) a bazooka
b) a bow and arrow
c) a slingshot
d) a spear

Pages 147–148 Pages 159–160 Pages 171–172 Pages 183–184

Level 3

What prophet saw a "wheel in the middle of a wheel"?

a) Ezekiel
b) Daniel
c) Haggai
d) Zechariah

Bronze

According to the book of Revelation, what is the number of "The Beast"?

a) 13
b) 57
c) 666
d) 1,000

Level 5

According to the apostle John, "God is" what?

a) power
b) love
c) wisdom
d) grace

Level 6

How long did Jesus fast before His temptation by Satan?

a) three days
b) a week
c) three weeks
d) forty days

Pages 149–152 Pages 161–164 Pages 173–176 Pages 185–188

Level 7

According to the apostle John, the traitor Judas Iscariot was also what?

a) an adulterer
b) a liar
c) a thief
d) a murderer

Silver

How did Jesus describe His "yoke"?

a) comfortable
b) loose
c) easy
d) pleasant

Level 9

According to Jesus, where is a prophet "without honor"?

a) in the synagogue
b) in his own house
c) in Samaria
d) in this world

Pages 153–155 Pages 165–167 Pages 177–179 Pages 189–191

Level 10

What did Paul suggest Timothy should take for his frequent illnesses?

a) wine
b) cheese
c) honey
d) herbs

Level 11

What did a seraph touch to Isaiah's lips to take away his guilt and sin?

a) a golden bowl
b) a budding pole
c) a live coal
d) a sealed scroll

Gold

Which famous Bible character shared his name with a lesser-known biblical woman?

a) Adam
b) Daniel
c) Moses
d) Noah

Pages 156–158 Pages 168–170 Pages 180–182 Pages 192–194

BIBLE TRIVIA

THIRTY INTERACTIVE QUIZZES THAT PUT YOU IN THE HOT SEAT

QUIZ 15

LEVEL 1

What Old Testament character received a "coat of many colors" from his doting father?

a) Adam
b) Joseph
c) Job
d) Goliath

LEVEL 2

Who was crucified with Jesus?

a) Peter
b) two robbers
c) a murderer
d) two insurrectionists

Pages 147–148 Pages 159–160 Pages 171–172 Pages 183–184

Level 3

Which of the following siblings does the Bible identify as twins?

a) Moses and Aaron
b) Jacob and Esau
c) Peter and Andrew
d) Mary and Martha

Bronze

The apostle Paul compared the Christian life to what sporting event?

a) a wrestling match
b) a race
c) weight lifting
d) gymnastics

Level 5

What was Cain's flippant response when God asked him where Abel was?

a) "Why would I care?"
b) "Find him yourself."
c) "I don't know anyone named Abel."
d) "Am I my brother's keeper?"

Pages 149–151 Pages 161–163 Pages 173–175 Pages 185–187

LEVEL 6

How many wives did King Solomon have?

a) one
b) thirty
c) one hundred
d) seven hundred

LEVEL 7

How did the sign on Jesus' cross describe Him?

a) "Traitor to Rome"
b) "The King of the Jews"
c) "The Blasphemer"
d) "Son of a Virgin"

SILVER

What is the name of the fourth horseman in the book of Revelation?

a) Pestilence
b) Death
c) War
d) Famine

LEVEL 9

What was Jesus discussing when He mentioned the name of Caesar?

a) the fall of Rome
b) idolatry
c) paying taxes
d) unjust leadership

Pages 152–155 Pages 164–167 Pages 176–179 Pages 188–191

Level 10

According to James, what is "friendship with the world"?

a) a grievous sin
b) hatred toward God
c) a poisonous viper
d) the foolishness of man

Level 11

Whose spirit did King Saul seek when consulting with the witch of Endor?

a) Moses'
b) Joshua's
c) Eli's
d) Samuel's

Gold

Which of the following does the Bible *not* list as a gate in the wall of Jerusalem?

a) Valley Gate
b) Dung Gate
c) Lion Gate
d) Fountain Gate

Pages 156–158 Pages 168–170 Pages 180–182 Pages 192–194

QUIZ 16

LEVEL 1

In what town was Jesus born?

a) Bethlehem
b) Ephesus
c) Rome
d) Philadelphia

LEVEL 2

What woman led to Samson's downfall?

a) Herodias
b) Jezebel
c) Delilah
d) Tokyo Rose

Pages 147–148 Pages 159–160 Pages 171–172 Pages 183–184

LEVEL 3

According to John, what was "in the beginning"?

a) nothing
b) the heavens and the earth
c) the Spirit
d) the Word

BRONZE

In response to God's offer, what one thing did Solomon request?

a) wealth
b) honor
c) wisdom
d) long life

LEVEL 5

According to Jeremiah, where does one go to find balm?

a) Babylon
b) Jerusalem
c) Gilead
d) Beersheba

LEVEL 6

In the "Triumphal Entry," how did Jesus enter Jerusalem?

a) on foot
b) on a white horse
c) on a donkey
d) in a golden chariot

Pages 149–152 Pages 161–164 Pages 173–176 Pages 185–188

Level 7

Which son of David was known for his exceptional good looks?

a) Amnon
b) Absalom
c) Adonijah
d) Ithream

Silver

Who wove the crown of thorns that Jesus wore?

a) Pontius Pilate
b) Caiaphas, the high priest
c) Herod
d) Roman soldiers

Level 9

According to the Proverbs, what has the power of life and death?

a) the tongue
b) the king
c) the rich
d) the heart

Pages 153–155 Pages 165–167 Pages 177–179 Pages 189–191

Level 10

Who initially resisted Elijah's suggestion that he wash seven times in the Jordan River to cure his leprosy?

a) Ben-Hadad
b) Gehazi
c) Naaman
d) Zedekiah

Level 11

Which disciple was so well known for his healing powers that people hoped to be touched by his shadow?

a) Paul
b) Philip
c) Peter
d) Stephen

Gold

Who was the well-known brother of Lahmi?

a) King Saul
b) Goliath
c) Gideon
d) Nebuchadnezzar

Pages 156–158 Pages 168–170 Pages 180–182 Pages 192–194

THIRTY INTERACTIVE QUIZZES THAT PUT YOU IN THE HOT SEAT

BIBLE TRIVIA

QUIZ 17

LEVEL 1

What led the wise men to the baby Jesus?

a) a billboard
b) a dove
c) a cloud
d) a star

LEVEL 2

Which of the following was Abraham's wife?

a) Mary Lincoln
b) Sarah
c) Rebekah
d) Rachel

Pages 147–148 Pages 159–160 Pages 171–172 Pages 183–184

LEVEL 3

In the Lord's Prayer, which phrase immediately follows "Our Father in heaven"?

a) "Give us today our daily bread"
b) "Lead us not into temptation"
c) "Hallowed be your name"
d) "Forgive us our debts"

BRONZE

What do the righteous (or just) live by?

a) faith
b) godly power
c) truth
d) the Spirit's strength

LEVEL 5

The Word of God is sharper than what?

a) a spear
b) a double-edged sword
c) a needle
d) a polished flint

Pages 149–151 Pages 161–163 Pages 173–175 Pages 185–187

Level 6

Which one of the following animals were Israelites permitted to eat?

a) pig
b) camel
c) cow
d) rabbit

Level 7

What did Paul tell Christians to "set your minds [or affection] on"?

a) things above
b) the scriptures
c) prayer
d) holiness

Silver

Where did Jesus say His followers would never walk?

a) in sin
b) in sorrow
c) in darkness
d) in fear

Level 9

Where were two of Christ's followers going when the resurrected Jesus joined them on the road?

a) Emmaus
b) Jerusalem
c) Samaria
d) Rome

Pages 152–155 Pages 164–167 Pages 176–179 Pages 188–191

Level 10

How did the Roman soldiers hasten the deaths of the robbers crucified with Jesus?

a) by giving them poison
b) by cutting off their heads
c) by spearing them
d) by breaking their legs

Level 11

Which of the following precious stones is *not* part of the New Jerusalem's foundation?

a) diamond
b) sapphire
c) emerald
d) amethyst

Gold

By what other name was the apostle Thomas known?

a) Didymus
b) Bithynia
c) Tychicus
d) Aenon

Pages 156–158 Pages 168–170 Pages 180–182 Pages 192–194

Quiz 18

Level 1

Where did Mary and Joseph place the newborn baby Jesus?

a) in a basket
b) in a crib
c) in a manger
d) on a sheep

Level 2

What was "manna"?

a) an Israelite rock band
b) a disease
c) a type of food
d) a sacred scroll

Pages 147–148 Pages 159–160 Pages 171–172 Pages 183–184

LEVEL 3

What animal did Aaron fashion a golden idol to represent?

a) a calf
b) an eagle
c) a snake
d) a lion

BRONZE

Which of the following statements did Jesus make just before He died on the cross?

a) "It is painful."
b) "It is unfair."
c) "It is finished."
d) "It is necessary."

LEVEL 5

According to Paul, who intercedes for Christians with "groans that words cannot express"?

a) the angels
b) Jesus
c) saints in heaven
d) the Spirit

LEVEL 6

Who was "a voice of one calling in the desert"?

a) John the Baptist
b) Jesus
c) Ezekiel
d) Haggai

Pages 149–152 Pages 161–164 Pages 173–176 Pages 185–188

LEVEL 7

What Roman official asked Jesus to heal his servant?

a) a centurion
b) a general
c) the proconsul
d) the governor

SILVER

What did John the Baptist say he was unworthy of doing for Christ?

a) bearing His name
b) untying His sandals
c) performing His ministry
d) cooking His supper

LEVEL 9

To which of the following did Jesus not liken the kingdom of heaven?

a) a fish net
b) a wedding banquet
c) a fire
d) a hidden treasure

Pages 153–155 Pages 165–167 Pages 177–179 Pages 189–191

LEVEL 10

How much time passed between Jesus' resurrection and His ascension into heaven?

a) three days
b) a week
c) forty days
d) a year

LEVEL 11

How long did Methuselah, the oldest man, live?

a) 130 years
b) 600 years
c) 969 years
d) 1,421 years

GOLD

Who is known as the "father of all who play the harp"?

a) David
b) Jubal
c) Seth
d) Asaph

Pages 156–158 Pages 168–170 Pages 180–182 Pages 192–194

THIRTY INTERACTIVE QUIZZES THAT PUT YOU IN THE HOT SEAT

BIBLE TRIVIA

QUIZ 19

LEVEL 1

What man did God use to lead the Israelites out of the Egyptian Pharaoh's bondage?

a) Adam
b) Jeremiah
c) Moses
d) Lawrence of Arabia

LEVEL 2

How did the animals enter Noah's ark?

a) single file
b) in pairs
c) in groups of five
d) they miraculously materialized inside

Pages 147–148 Pages 159–160 Pages 171–172 Pages 183–184

Level 3

What was the name of the man from whom Jesus cast many evil spirits?

a) Army
b) Legion
c) Squadron
d) Troop

Bronze

What physical ailment did Paul have temporarily after his conversion experience?

a) leprosy
b) lameness
c) deafness
d) blindness

Level 5

How quickly will the glorification of the saints, announced by "the last trumpet," take place?

a) in the twinkling of an eye
b) as a horse gallops
c) in a heartbeat
d) as the eagle swoops

Pages 149–151 Pages 161–163 Pages 173–175 Pages 185–187

Level 6

The disciples received the Holy Spirit during what special holiday?

a) the Day of Atonement
b) Pentecost
c) Passover
d) the Feast of Purim

Level 7

Where was Saul of Tarsus when he was converted to Christianity?

a) atop Mars Hill
b) on the Mediterranean Sea
c) in Jerusalem
d) near Damascus

Silver

Complete Jesus' statement about human souls: "The harvest is plentiful. . ."

a) "and the time is short."
b) "but the workers are few."
c) "for the Lord has blessed."
d) "with the choicest of fruit."

Pages 152–154 Pages 164–166 Pages 176–178 Pages 188–190

Level 9

What word did the crowds repeat during Jesus' triumphal entry into Jerusalem?

a) "Hosanna"
c) "Holy"
b) "Hallelujah"
d) "Honor"

Level 10

On what island was the apostle John when he experienced his Revelation?

a) Crete
c) Sicily
b) Patmos
d) Cyprus

Level 11

What king literally saw "the handwriting on the wall"?

a) Uzziah
b) Nebuchadnezzar
c) Belshazzar
d) Darius

Gold

Who was the husband of the prophetess Deborah?

a) Lappidoth
c) Ehud
b) Sisera
d) Jabin

Pages 155–158 Pages 167–170 Pages 179–182 Pages 191–194

QUIZ 20

LEVEL 1

What Old Testament prophet spent a night in a lions' den?

a) Jeremiah
b) Daniel
c) Joel
d) Habakkuk

LEVEL 2

By interpreting Pharaoh's dreams, Joseph was able to prepare Egypt for what disaster?

a) famine
b) flood
c) earthquake
d) stock market crash

Pages 147–148 Pages 159–160 Pages 171–172 Pages 183–184

LEVEL 3

What is the name of the archangel mentioned in scripture?

a) Michael
b) Benjamin
c) Gabriel
d) Donatello

BRONZE

What Old Testament figure wrestled with God?

a) Abraham
b) Isaac
c) Jacob
d) Moses

LEVEL 5

How did Samuel know that Saul had disobeyed God by failing to completely annihilate the Amalekites?

a) Saul's shifty eyes
b) the sound of livestock
c) Amalekite military stragglers
d) the Urim and Thummim

LEVEL 6

What did a dove bring back to the ark, indicating to Noah that the great floodwaters had receded?

a) a worm
b) a dead fish
c) a head of grain
d) an olive leaf

Pages 149–152 Pages 161–164 Pages 173–176 Pages 185–188

Level 7

What sound accompanied the Holy Spirit's arrival at Pentecost?

a) a trumpet blast
b) a violent wind
c) a shout of joy
d) an angel choir

Silver

According to the apostle Paul, there is no what for "those who are in Christ Jesus"?

a) condemnation
b) fear of death
c) pain and sorrow
d) sinful desire

Level 9

According to Jesus, what was Satan "from the beginning"?

a) a deceiver
b) a rebel
c) an enemy
d) a murderer

Pages 153–155 Pages 165–167 Pages 177–179 Pages 189–191

LEVEL 10

Isaiah prophesied of a time when the nations would beat their swords into what?

a) plowshares
b) anvils
c) goblets
d) the ground

LEVEL 11

When King Xerxes chose Esther as his queen, whom did she replace?

a) Vashti
b) Athaliah
c) Jezebel
d) Bathsheba

GOLD

On what mount did King Saul die?

a) Nebo
b) Carmel
c) Hermon
d) Gilboa

Pages 156–158 Pages 168–170 Pages 180–182 Pages 192–194

BIBLE TRIVIA

THIRTY INTERACTIVE QUIZZES THAT PUT YOU IN THE HOT SEAT

QUIZ 21

LEVEL 1

To which of the following animals are Christians compared?

a) hamsters
b) camels
c) sheep
d) elephants

LEVEL 2

What was the name of the angel who told Mary she would give birth to Jesus?

a) Solomon
b) Rafael
c) Gabriel
d) Alexander

Pages 147–148 Pages 159–160 Pages 171–172 Pages 183–184

Level 3

According to David, God's spiritual cleansing makes us whiter than what?

a) dried bones
b) snow
c) clouds
d) wool

Bronze

What was Matthew's occupation before he became a disciple of Jesus?

a) fisherman
b) merchant
c) physician
d) tax collector

Level 5

According the apostle Paul, the Christian's body is the *what* of the Holy Spirit?

a) temple
b) house
c) chariot
d) slave

Pages 149–151 Pages 161–163 Pages 173–175 Pages 185–187

Level 6

According to Ecclesiastes, when should you "remember your Creator"?

a) "in the days of your youth"
b) "when times of trouble come"
c) "as your years increase"
d) "in joy and in sorrow"

Level 7

What disguise does Satan use to try to fool Christians?

a) a passionate preacher
b) a wounded traveler
c) an angel of light
d) an innocent child

Silver

According to the Proverbs, what is "good medicine"?

a) the word of God
b) a good friend
c) a cheerful heart
d) a generous spirit

Level 9

Which prophet was the son of Hannah and Elkanah?

a) Zechariah
b) Samuel
c) Elijah
d) Nathan

Pages 152–155 Pages 164–167 Pages 176–179 Pages 188–191

LEVEL 10

Where did God instruct Abraham to sacrifice his son Isaac?

a) Sodom
b) Bethel
c) the Red Sea
d) Moriah

LEVEL 11

For what offense did Elisha curse some young people of Bethel, resulting in the mauling of forty-two youth by bears?

a) desecrating the Temple
b) using the Lord's name in vain
c) immorality
d) making fun of his baldness

GOLD

What current event did Jesus use as an example to emphasize the need for repentance?

a) an earthquake in Jerusalem
b) a tower collapse that killed eighteen people
c) an outbreak of the plague
d) the drowning of seven people in a boat accident

Pages 156–158 Pages 168–170 Pages 180–182 Pages 192–194

QUIZ 22

Level 1

Why was Jesus' birth to Mary miraculous?

a) She was very old.
b) She was barren.
c) She was a virgin.
d) She already had twenty-two other children.

Level 2

What was the punishment for Lot's wife, who looked back on the destruction of Sodom and Gomorrah?

a) She contracted leprosy.
b) She was struck blind.
c) She lost her firstborn son.
d) She became a pillar of salt.

Pages 147–148 Pages 159–160 Pages 171–172 Pages 183–184

LEVEL 3

What kind of branches did people spread before Jesus during His "triumphal entry" into Jerusalem?

a) olive
b) oak
c) palm
d) sycamore

BRONZE

Where did Jesus send the evil spirits He cast out of a man called "Legion"?

a) into the desert
b) into a herd of pigs
c) into the tombs
d) straight into hell

LEVEL 5

What did Jesus say would not prevail against His church?

a) the sins of mankind
b) the armies of Satan
c) the gates of Hades
d) the forces of evil

LEVEL 6

Whom did Jesus physically drive out of the Temple?

a) scribes
b) Pharisees
c) money changers
d) Roman soldiers

Pages 149–152 Pages 161–164 Pages 173–176 Pages 185–188

Level 7

According to James, what should a tempted person never say?

a) "The devil made me do it."
b) "My own strength shall save me."
c) "It is of little account."
d) "God is tempting me."

Silver

Which of the following sounds will *not* accompany Jesus' Second Coming?

a) the trumpet of God
b) mighty hoof beats
c) the voice of the archangel
d) a loud command

Level 9

According to the Proverbs, what is worthless "in the day of wrath"?

a) power
b) wealth
c) fame
d) idols

Pages 153–155 Pages 165–167 Pages 177–179 Pages 189–191

Level 10

Which of the following was *not* one of Job's "comforters"?

a) Eliphaz the Temanite
b) Bildad the Shuhite
c) Zophar the Naamathite
d) Hamor the Hivite

Level 11

Of what was Bartimaeus healed?

a) leprosy
b) demon possession
c) blindness
d) lameness

Gold

As the book of Acts concludes, where in Rome is the apostle Paul?

a) Caesar's palace
b) a dungeon
c) the Forum
d) a rented house

Pages 156–158 Pages 168–170 Pages 180–182 Pages 192–194

THIRTY INTERACTIVE QUIZZES THAT PUT YOU IN THE HOT SEAT

BIBLE TRIVIA

QUIZ 23

LEVEL 1

Jesus said, "I am the good" what?

a) beekeeper
b) shepherd
c) fisherman
d) camel driver

LEVEL 2

According to Jesus, who will inherit the earth?

a) the environmentalists
b) the merciful
c) the peacemakers
d) the meek

Pages 147–148 Pages 159–160 Pages 171–172 Pages 183–184

LEVEL 3

After the Fall, what did God place around the Tree of Life to keep Adam and Eve away?

a) hungry lions
b) a tall fence
c) cherubim with flaming swords
d) a deep moat

BRONZE

According to the Proverbs, a gentle answer turns away what?

a) wrath
b) enemies
c) arguments
d) lawsuits

LEVEL 5

What name did Jesus give to Simon Peter?

a) Apollos
b) Cephas
c) Demas
d) Festus

LEVEL 6

Whom did the widow Ruth marry?

a) Jesse
b) Boaz
c) Elimelech
d) Obed

Pages 149–152 Pages 161–164 Pages 173–176 Pages 185–188

LEVEL 7

According to Micah, where does God place forgiven sins?

a) beyond the stars
b) the pit of hell
c) the depths of the sea
d) gloomy dungeons

SILVER

What were John the Baptist's clothes made of?

a) fine silk
b) white linen
c) woven yarn
d) camel hair

LEVEL 9

Where did Jonah try to go to avoid God's call to preach?

a) Nineveh
b) Babylon
c) Joppa
d) Tarshish

Pages 153–155 Pages 165–167 Pages 177–179 Pages 189–191

LEVEL 10

What convinced the apostle Paul to take the gospel message to Macedonia?

a) God's audible voice
b) a vision of a man requesting help
c) a letter from Peter
d) a sign in the sky

LEVEL 11

What is Jesus' last statement in the Bible?

a) "Continue in my love."
b) "Remember the Lord your God."
c) "I am coming soon."
d) "My Father's house awaits you."

GOLD

Who became king of Judah at age eight and was commended for turning to God "with all his heart...soul...and strength"?

a) Josiah
b) Amon
c) Manasseh
d) Zedekiah

Pages 156–158 Pages 168–170 Pages 180–182 Pages 192–194

QUIZ 24

LEVEL 1

What substance did Jesus miraculously walk upon?

a) water
b) clouds
c) fire
d) eggshells

LEVEL 2

When did it happen that "God created the heavens and the earth"?

a) "Billions of years ago. . ."
b) "In the fullness of time. . ."
c) "In the beginning. . ."
d) "From ancient times. . ."

Pages 147–148 Pages 159–160 Pages 171–172 Pages 183–184

Level 3

What instrument did David play to soothe King Saul's spirit?

a) flute
b) harp
c) harmonium
d) tambourine

Bronze

According to the apostle Paul, the Thessalonians were to "greet all the brothers with a holy" what?

a) hug
b) kiss
c) handshake
d) blessing

Level 5

Complete this quotation of Jesus: "Foxes have holes and birds of the air have nests, but the Son of Man..."

a) "has a beautiful palace in heaven."
b) "has a small home in Jerusalem."
c) "has no place to lay His head."
d) "has twelve disciples to live with."

Level 6

How did Jesus say He was sending out His disciples?

a) like doves among hawks
b) like sheep among wolves
c) like travelers among thieves
d) like children among bears

x2 Pages 149–152 Pages 161–164 Pages 173–176 Pages 185–188

Level 7

What prophet took an adulterous wife as a symbol of Israel's unfaithfulness?

a) Daniel
b) Hosea
c) Joel
d) Amos

Silver

In his Revelation, what did John see sitting upon a scarlet beast?

a) a king
b) a priest
c) a prostitute
d) a demon

Level 9

According to Matthew, what phenomenon accompanied both the death and resurrection of Jesus?

a) lightning
b) howling wind
c) an earthquake
d) an eclipse

Pages 153–155 Pages 165–167 Pages 177–179 Pages 189–191

Level 10

What did the prophet Elisha request from his mentor, the prophet Elijah?

a) a double portion of God's Spirit
b) a scroll of instructions
c) his sandals
d) one month together in private

Level 11

Who assisted Joseph of Arimathea in preparing Jesus' body for burial?

a) Zacchaeus
b) Bartimaeus
c) Cornelius
d) Nicodemus

Gold

What young man fell from a window and died during a long message by Paul?

a) Eutychus
b) Demetrius
c) Erastus
d) Crispus

Pages 156–158 Pages 168–170 Pages 180–182 Pages 192–194

THIRTY INTERACTIVE QUIZZES THAT PUT YOU IN THE HOT SEAT

BIBLE TRIVIA

QUIZ 25

LEVEL 1

Jesus said, "I am the" *what* "of life"?

a) vitamins
b) meat
c) wine
d) bread

LEVEL 2

What city's wall collapsed at the shout of Joshua's army?

a) Jericho
b) Babylon
c) Jerusalem
d) Beijing

Pages 147–148 Pages 159–160 Pages 171–172 Pages 183–184

Level 3

What does the shortest verse in the Bible say Jesus did?

a) smiled
b) wept
c) prayed
d) spoke

Bronze

What kind of seed did Jesus compare to the kingdom of God?

a) pomegranate
b) grape
c) mustard
d) olive

Level 5

According to the Proverbs, where should lazy people go for wisdom?

a) the library
b) the temple
c) a wheat field
d) the ant

Level 6

According to the apostle Paul, in trials and hardships Christians are "more than" what?

a) conquerors
b) angels
c) warriors
d) kings

Pages 149–152 Pages 161–164 Pages 173–176 Pages 185–188

Level 7

How many righteous people did the city of Sodom need to keep God from destroying it?

a) one thousand
b) two hundred
c) fifty
d) ten

Silver

What man did David have killed in order to take his wife, Bathsheba?

a) Uriah
b) Joab
c) Ziba
d) Benaiah

Level 9

Whose mother-in-law had a fever healed by Jesus?

a) Thomas
b) Simon Peter
c) Matthew
d) Judas Iscariot

Pages 153–155 Pages 165–167 Pages 177–179 Pages 189–191

Level 10

Which minor prophet prophesied that the Messiah would be born in Bethlehem?

a) Joel
b) Amos
c) Micah
d) Zechariah

Level 11

What follower of Jesus met the resurrected Christ on the road to Emmaus?

a) Thomas
b) Nathanael
c) Martha
d) Cleopas

Gold

Why did Pilate's wife advise her husband to leave Jesus alone?

a) She believed Isaiah's prophecies.
b) She had seen Jesus perform miracles.
c) She had had a bad dream.
d) She feared a Galilean revolt.

Pages 156–158 Pages 168–170 Pages 180–182 Pages 192–194

Quiz 26

Level 1

What crafty animal convinced Eve to eat the forbidden fruit?

a) cow
b) dove
c) serpent
d) dinosaur

Level 2

What kind of water did Jesus offer the Samaritan woman at the well?

a) living
b) cool
c) fresh
d) purified

Pages 147–148 Pages 159–160 Pages 171–172 Pages 183–184

LEVEL 3

Complete this quotation of Jesus: "Then you will know the truth. . ."

a) "and the truth will set you free."
b) "and you will be wise."
c) "and many will accept your teaching."
d) "and you will enjoy prosperity."

BRONZE

According to the book of Ephesians, it is by *what* that we are saved?

a) good works
b) grace
c) love
d) tithing

LEVEL 5

What was the reaction of ninety-year-old Sarah when the Lord said she would bear a son?

a) She laughed.
b) She wept.
c) She fainted.
d) She argued.

Pages 149–151 Pages 161–163 Pages 173–175 Pages 185–187

LEVEL 6

Which of the following baking items did Jesus compare to the kingdom of heaven?

a) a pan
b) flour
c) an egg
d) yeast

LEVEL 7

What did Pharaoh and the Egyptians force their Israelite slaves to produce?

a) armor
b) wagons
c) bricks
d) idols

SILVER

On which day of creation did God make birds and fish?

a) day two
b) day three
c) day four
d) day five

LEVEL 9

Where were the disciples first called "Christians"?

a) Antioch
b) Cyprus
c) Jerusalem
d) Pamphylia

Pages 152–155 Pages 164–167 Pages 176–179 Pages 188–191

Level 10

Who initially scoffed at Jesus, saying, "Nazareth! Can anything good come from there?"

a) Peter
b) Philip
c) John
d) Nathanael

Level 11

What sin of David led to a plague that killed seventy thousand Israelites?

a) his adultery with Bathsheba
b) the murder of Uriah
c) counting the Israelites
d) polygamy

Gold

What famous Bible personality did God name "Jedidiah"?

a) Noah
b) Solomon
c) Jeremiah
d) Daniel

Pages 156–158 Pages 168–170 Pages 180–182 Pages 192–194

THIRTY INTERACTIVE QUIZZES THAT PUT YOU IN THE HOT SEAT

BIBLE TRIVIA

Quiz 27

Level 1

Which of the following is *not* a biblical nationality?

a) Canaanite
b) Perizzite
c) Jebusite
d) Woolite

Level 2

Which of the following was *not* a gift the wise men brought the baby Jesus?

a) gold
b) diamonds
c) frankincense
d) myrrh

Pages 147–148 Pages 159–160 Pages 171–172 Pages 183–184

Level 3

Jesus said, "I am the way, the truth, and the" what?

a) life
c) door
b) bread
d) Lord

Bronze

How did John the Baptist die?

a) by crucifixion
b) by beheading
c) by stoning
d) by being torn apart by animals

Level 5

Potiphar's wife tried to seduce what Old Testament character?

a) Joshua
c) Jacob
b) Judah
d) Joseph

Level 6

Who had a vision of heaven as he was being martyred for his strong preaching?

a) Stephen
c) Paul
b) Matthias
d) Timothy

Pages 149–152 Pages 161–164 Pages 173–176 Pages 185–188

Level 7

According to the book of Romans, how did God prove His love for sinners?

a) Noah's rainbow
b) Christ's death
c) Paul's conversion
d) John's Revelation

Silver

What prophet rebuked David for his sin with Bathsheba?

a) Samuel
b) Iddo
c) Nathan
d) Jehu

Level 9

Where did Jesus say Peter would find a coin to pay their temple tax?

a) along the roadside
b) in a fish's mouth
c) in the hem of Peter's robe
d) on the floor of the Upper Room

Pages 153–155 Pages 165–167 Pages 177–179 Pages 189–191

Level 10

What man blessed Mary and Joseph as they presented the young Jesus to the Lord?

a) Phanuel
b) Simeon
c) Heli
d) Jairus

Level 11

Who was stoned to death after taking silver and gold from the destroyed city of Jericho?

a) Achan
b) Balak
c) Jephunneh
d) Zelophehad

Gold

What does the name "Barnabas" mean?

a) Devoted to God
b) Son of Encouragement
c) The Lord Saves
d) Man of Faith

Pages 156–158 Pages 168–170 Pages 180–182 Pages 192–194

QUIZ 28

LEVEL 1

From what substance did God form Adam?

a) chopped figs
b) water
c) dust
d) grass

LEVEL 2

On what did God inscribe His Ten Commandments?

a) a compact disc
b) papyrus
c) stone tablets
d) a leather scroll

Pages 147–148 Pages 159–160 Pages 171–172 Pages 183–184

Level 3

Jesus said that He is the Alpha and the what?

a) Beta
b) Delta
c) Omega
d) Sigma

Bronze

For the apostle Paul, "to live is Christ, and to die is" what?

a) gain
b) joy
c) peace
d) heaven

Level 5

How many churches did Jesus address in the book of Revelation?

a) one
b) three
c) seven
d) twenty-one

Level 6

Which disciples asked to sit at Jesus' right and left hand in heaven?

a) James and John
b) Philip and Thomas
c) Peter and Andrew
d) Matthew and Simon the Zealot

Pages 149–152 Pages 161–164 Pages 173–176 Pages 185–188

LEVEL 7

What woman, a seller of purple cloth, was one of the first Christian converts in Philippi?

a) Lydia
b) Sapphira
c) Susanna
d) Persis

SILVER

According to the Psalms, what is "the beginning of wisdom"?

a) the prayer of faith
b) obedience
c) the fear of the Lord
d) repentance

LEVEL 9

What brothers were known as "Boanerges," or "sons of thunder"?

a) Cain and Abel
b) Jacob and Esau
c) James and John
d) Peter and Andrew

Pages 153–155 Pages 165–167 Pages 177–179 Pages 189–191

Level 10

The Jewish celebration of Purim originated with which Bible story?

a) Esther and Mordecai
b) David and Goliath
c) Joshua and the battle of Jericho
d) Nehemiah and the walls of Jerusalem

Level 11

How many times was the apostle Paul shipwrecked?

a) none
b) once
c) three times
d) eight times

Gold

Who replaced Judas Iscariot as the twelfth apostle?

a) John Mark
b) Justus
c) Matthias
d) Luke

Pages 156–158 Pages 168–170 Pages 180–182 Pages 192–194

THIRTY INTERACTIVE QUIZZES THAT PUT YOU IN THE HOT SEAT

BIBLE TRIVIA

QUIZ 29

LEVEL 1

Which of the following does the Bible say God keeps numbered?

a) the hairs of your head
b) the trees of the forest
c) the fish of the sea
d) the burgers served at McDonalds

LEVEL 2

What was the "forbidden fruit" that Adam and Eve ate?

a) an apple
b) a fig
c) a pear
d) it's not specified

Pages 147–148 Pages 159–160 Pages 171–172 Pages 183–184

Level 3

What signal did Judas Iscariot use to betray Jesus to His enemies?

a) a kiss
b) a hug
c) a handshake
d) a nod

Bronze

Who sold his birthright for a meal of bread and lentil stew?

a) Jacob
b) Laban
c) Isaac
d) Esau

Level 5

What man was also known by the name "Israel"?

a) Adam
b) Moses
c) Jacob
d) David

Level 6

What was Jesus' first miracle?

a) healing a blind man
b) raising Lazarus from the dead
c) walking on water
d) turning water into wine

Pages 149–152 Pages 161–164 Pages 173–176 Pages 185–188

LEVEL 7

According to James, faith without what is dead or useless?

a) love
b) prayer
c) God
d) deeds

SILVER

What immoral woman is commended in the book of Hebrews for her faith?

a) Gomer
b) Rahab
c) Jezebel
d) the woman at the well

LEVEL 9

In addition to Jesus, who did the chief priests want to put to death?

a) Peter
b) John
c) Lazarus
d) Nicodemus

Pages 153–155 Pages 165–167 Pages 177–179 Pages 189–191

Level 10

When Paul said, "I wish that all men were as I am," he was wishing that they were what?

a) apostles
b) missionaries
c) disciplined
d) unmarried

Level 11

Which of the following is *not* a food the Israelites craved from Egypt?

a) cucumbers
b) melons
c) onions
d) apples

Gold

What judge of Israel made a rash vow that led to the sacrifice of his only daughter?

a) Othniel
b) Jephthah
c) Shamgar
d) Samson

Pages 156–158 Pages 168–170 Pages 180–182 Pages 192–194

QUIZ 30

LEVEL 1

From what part of Adam did God form Eve?

a) a thigh bone
b) a rib
c) a finger
d) an ear lobe

LEVEL 2

What sacrificial animal shares its name with Jesus?

a) bull
b) dove
c) ram
d) lamb

Pages 147–148 Pages 159–160 Pages 171–172 Pages 183–184

LEVEL 3

Whose temple offering was commended by Jesus?

a) a wealthy Pharisee's
b) a young child's
c) a beloved priest's
d) a poor widow's

BRONZE

Where did Solomon obtain the cedar with which he built the Lord's Temple?

a) Lebanon
b) Sinai
c) Egypt
d) Cyprus

LEVEL 5

What ruler tried to eliminate the baby Jesus by ordering the murder of all boys two years old and younger around Bethlehem?

a) Caesar Augustus
b) Tiberius Caesar
c) Pontius Pilate
d) Herod

Pages 149–151 Pages 161–163 Pages 173–175 Pages 185–187

Level 6

When the Holy Spirit descended on Jesus after His baptism, how did it appear?

a) like a sparrow
b) like a dove
c) like an eagle
d) like a snowflake

Level 7

What was the name of the boy that Abram fathered by Sarai's maidservant Hagar?

a) Ishmael
b) Isaac
c) Issachar
d) Isaiah

Silver

What is the name of the female judge who led Israel to a victory over the Canaanites?

a) Hannah
b) Deborah
c) Abigail
d) Huldah

Level 9

According to Paul, how many people saw Jesus after His resurrection?

a) one
b) twelve
c) twenty-seven
d) more than five hundred

x2 Pages 152–155 | Pages 164–167 | Pages 176–179 | Pages 188–191

Level 10

Where did Jesus move after leaving Nazareth?

a) Capernaum
b) Jerusalem
c) Cana
d) Bethany

Level 11

What prophet was thrown into a muddy pit for his discouraging messages?

a) Obadiah
b) Nahum
c) Jeremiah
d) Zephaniah

Gold

What builder's tool did God show Amos to indicate Israel's coming judgment?

a) a chisel
b) a hammer
c) a trowel
d) a plumb line

Pages 156–158 Pages 168–170 Pages 180–182 Pages 192–194

Bonuses

DOUBLE YOUR CHANCES

LEVEL 1

INCORRECT ANSWERS INCLUDE:

Quiz 1—A and D
Quiz 2—B and D
Quiz 3—C and D
Quiz 4—A and B
Quiz 5—B and D
Quiz 6—C and D
Quiz 7—A and D
Quiz 8—C and D
Quiz 9—A and B
Quiz 10—A and D
Quiz 11—B and C
Quiz 12—A and D
Quiz 13—C and D
Quiz 14—A and B
Quiz 15—A and D
Quiz 16—B and D
Quiz 17—A and B
Quiz 18—B and D
Quiz 19—A and D
Quiz 20—A and C
Quiz 21—A and D
Quiz 22—B and D
Quiz 23—A and D
Quiz 24—C and D
Quiz 25—A and C
Quiz 26—A and D
Quiz 27—A and B
Quiz 28—A and B
Quiz 29—C and D
Quiz 30—A and D

Double Your Chances

Level 2

Incorrect answers include:

Quiz 1—A and D
Quiz 2—A and B
Quiz 3—C and D
Quiz 4—A and C
Quiz 5—C and D
Quiz 6—A and D
Quiz 7—A and C
Quiz 8—A and B
Quiz 9—C and D
Quiz 10—A and C
Quiz 11—B and D
Quiz 12—A and D
Quiz 13—A and B
Quiz 14—A and D
Quiz 15—A and C
Quiz 16—B and D
Quiz 17—A and D
Quiz 18—A and B
Quiz 19—C and D
Quiz 20—B and D
Quiz 21—A and D
Quiz 22—B and C
Quiz 23—A and C
Quiz 24—A and D
Quiz 25—C and D
Quiz 26—B and D
Quiz 27—C and D
Quiz 28—A and B
Quiz 29—B and C
Quiz 30—A and C

Double Your Chances

Level 3

Incorrect answers include:

Quiz 1—B and C
Quiz 2—C and D
Quiz 3—A and D
Quiz 4—B and D
Quiz 5—B and D
Quiz 6—A and B
Quiz 7—A and C
Quiz 8—A and D
Quiz 9—A and C
Quiz 10—A and D
Quiz 11—B and C
Quiz 12—A and C
Quiz 13—B and C
Quiz 14—B and C
Quiz 15—A and C
Quiz 16—A and B
Quiz 17—B and D
Quiz 18—C and D
Quiz 19—A and C
Quiz 20—B and D
Quiz 21—A and D
Quiz 22—A and B
Quiz 23—B and D
Quiz 24—C and D
Quiz 25—A and D
Quiz 26—C and D
Quiz 27—B and C
Quiz 28—B and D
Quiz 29—C and D
Quiz 30—A and B

Double Your Chances

Bronze

Incorrect answers include:

Quiz 1—A and B
Quiz 2—A and D
Quiz 3—C and D
Quiz 4—A and C
Quiz 5—B and D
Quiz 6—A and D
Quiz 7—A and B
Quiz 8—C and D
Quiz 9—B and C
Quiz 10—C and D
Quiz 11—B and D
Quiz 12—A and C
Quiz 13—B and D
Quiz 14—B and D
Quiz 15—C and D
Quiz 16—A and B
Quiz 17—B and D
Quiz 18—B and D
Quiz 19—A and C
Quiz 20—B and D
Quiz 21—B and C
Quiz 22—C and D
Quiz 23—B and D
Quiz 24—A and C
Quiz 25—B and D
Quiz 26—A and D
Quiz 27—C and D
Quiz 28—B and C
Quiz 29—A and C
Quiz 30—C and D

Double Your Chances

Level 5

Incorrect answers include:

Quiz 1—B and D
Quiz 2—B and D
Quiz 3—A and D
Quiz 4—B and C
Quiz 5—B and D
Quiz 6—A and B
Quiz 7—C and D
Quiz 8—C and D
Quiz 9—B and C
Quiz 10—A and B
Quiz 11—B and C
Quiz 12—B and D
Quiz 13—B and C
Quiz 14—A and C
Quiz 15—A and B
Quiz 16—A and D
Quiz 17—C and D
Quiz 18—A and B
Quiz 19—B and D
Quiz 20—A and C
Quiz 21—C and D
Quiz 22—A and B
Quiz 23—A and D
Quiz 24—A and B
Quiz 25—A and B
Quiz 26—C and D
Quiz 27—A and B
Quiz 28—A and D
Quiz 29—A and B
Quiz 30—B and C

Double Your Chances

Level 6

Incorrect answers include:

Quiz 1—C and D
Quiz 2—B and D
Quiz 3—A and C
Quiz 4—B and C
Quiz 5—A and C
Quiz 6—A and B
Quiz 7—B and D
Quiz 8—A and D
Quiz 9—A and B
Quiz 10—C and D
Quiz 11—A and B
Quiz 12—A and D
Quiz 13—B and D
Quiz 14—B and C
Quiz 15—A and C
Quiz 16—A and B
Quiz 17—A and B
Quiz 18—C and D
Quiz 19—A and C
Quiz 20—A and B
Quiz 21—B and C
Quiz 22—A and D
Quiz 23—C and D
Quiz 24—A and C
Quiz 25—C and D
Quiz 26—A and B
Quiz 27—C and D
Quiz 28—B and D
Quiz 29—B and C
Quiz 30—C and D

Double Your Chances

Level 7

Incorrect answers include:

Quiz 1—A and D
Quiz 2—A and B
Quiz 3—C and D
Quiz 4—A and C
Quiz 5—A and D
Quiz 6—A and B
Quiz 7—C and D
Quiz 8—A and C
Quiz 9—C and D
Quiz 10—B and C
Quiz 11—A and B
Quiz 12—B and C
Quiz 13—B and D
Quiz 14—A and B
Quiz 15—A and D
Quiz 16—C and D
Quiz 17—B and C
Quiz 18—B and D
Quiz 19—A and B
Quiz 20—C and D
Quiz 21—B and D
Quiz 22—A and C
Quiz 23—A and D
Quiz 24—A and C
Quiz 25—B and C
Quiz 26—B and D
Quiz 27—C and D
Quiz 28—B and D
Quiz 29—B and C
Quiz 30—B and D

Double Your Chances

Silver

Incorrect answers include:

Quiz 1—C and D
Quiz 2—A and C
Quiz 3—A and B
Quiz 4—B and C
Quiz 5—B and C
Quiz 6—C and D
Quiz 7—A and B
Quiz 8—A and D
Quiz 9—C and D
Quiz 10—B and D
Quiz 11—A and C
Quiz 12—B and C
Quiz 13—B and D
Quiz 14—A and B
Quiz 15—A and C
Quiz 16—B and C
Quiz 17—B and D
Quiz 18—C and D
Quiz 19—A and D
Quiz 20—C and D
Quiz 21—B and D
Quiz 22—A and C
Quiz 23—A and B
Quiz 24—B and D
Quiz 25—B and C
Quiz 26—A and C
Quiz 27—A and D
Quiz 28—B and D
Quiz 29—A and C
Quiz 30—A and C

Double Your Chances

Level 9

Incorrect answers include:

Quiz 1—A and D
Quiz 2—C and D
Quiz 3—B and D
Quiz 4—A and B
Quiz 5—A and C
Quiz 6—B and D
Quiz 7—C and D
Quiz 8—A and B
Quiz 9—B and C
Quiz 10—B and D
Quiz 11—A and D
Quiz 12—B and C
Quiz 13—A and D
Quiz 14—C and D
Quiz 15—A and B
Quiz 16—C and D
Quiz 17—B and D
Quiz 18—B and D
Quiz 19—B and C
Quiz 20—A and B
Quiz 21—A and D
Quiz 22—C and D
Quiz 23—A and B
Quiz 24—B and D
Quiz 25—A and C
Quiz 26—B and D
Quiz 27—A and D
Quiz 28—A and B
Quiz 29—B and D
Quiz 30—A and C

Double Your Chances

Level 10

Incorrect answers include:

Quiz 1—C and D
Quiz 2—A and C
Quiz 3—A and D
Quiz 4—A and C
Quiz 5—B and D
Quiz 6—A and B
Quiz 7—C and D
Quiz 8—B and C
Quiz 9—B and D
Quiz 10—A and D
Quiz 11—B and D
Quiz 12—A and B
Quiz 13—A and C
Quiz 14—B and C
Quiz 15—A and D
Quiz 16—B and D
Quiz 17—A and B
Quiz 18—B and D
Quiz 19—C and D
Quiz 20—C and D
Quiz 21—A and B
Quiz 22—B and C
Quiz 23—C and D
Quiz 24—C and D
Quiz 25—A and B
Quiz 26—B and C
Quiz 27—C and D
Quiz 28—B and D
Quiz 29—A and C
Quiz 30—C and D

Double Your Chances

Level 11

Incorrect answers include:

Quiz 1—B and C
Quiz 2—C and D
Quiz 3—A and D
Quiz 4—B and D
Quiz 5—A and B
Quiz 6—B and C
Quiz 7—A and C
Quiz 8—C and D
Quiz 9—A and D
Quiz 10—B and C
Quiz 11—A and D
Quiz 12—B and D
Quiz 13—C and D
Quiz 14—A and B
Quiz 15—A and C
Quiz 16—B and D
Quiz 17—C and D
Quiz 18—B and D
Quiz 19—A and D
Quiz 20—C and D
Quiz 21—B and C
Quiz 22—A and D
Quiz 23—B and D
Quiz 24—B and C
Quiz 25—A and B
Quiz 26—B and D
Quiz 27—C and D
Quiz 28—A and D
Quiz 29—B and C
Quiz 30—A and B

Double Your Chances

Gold

Incorrect answers include:

Quiz 1—A and D
Quiz 2—A and C
Quiz 3—B and C
Quiz 4—C and D
Quiz 5—A and B
Quiz 6—B and D
Quiz 7—C and D
Quiz 8—A and D
Quiz 9—B and D
Quiz 10—B and C
Quiz 11—C and D
Quiz 12—B and C
Quiz 13—A and B
Quiz 14—A and C
Quiz 15—A and D
Quiz 16—C and D
Quiz 17—B and D
Quiz 18—C and D
Quiz 19—B and C
Quiz 20—A and C
Quiz 21—C and D
Quiz 22—B and C
Quiz 23—C and D
Quiz 24—B and C
Quiz 25—A and D
Quiz 26—A and D
Quiz 27—A and C
Quiz 28—B and D
Quiz 29—A and D
Quiz 30—A and C

Have a Hint

Level 1

Quiz 1—He's first alphabetically, too.
Quiz 2—You know a clue's in this sentence...
Quiz 3—King ______, Star of ______.
Quiz 4—Though she had the name, she was not "quite contrary."
Quiz 5—Good luck finding these posted on a school wall.
Quiz 6—Maybe he met her late in the day.
Quiz 7—Phone a buddy for help on this one...
Quiz 8—This is not a trick question—it's really that easy!
Quiz 9—If he's been portrayed by Charlton Heston, he's the one.
Quiz 10—And God said, "Don't sweat it."
Quiz 11—Don't you love a Sunday afternoon nap?
Quiz 12—With Jesus, they made a baker's dozen.
Quiz 13—He zigged, and zagged, and zipped through the crowd.
Quiz 14—A sensitive, sympathetic servant.
Quiz 15—He was "cool," not "sloppy."
Quiz 16—Starts like a common name of a girl.
Quiz 17—A certain celestial signal...
Quiz 18—Where there was no danger from a stranger...
Quiz 19—The Israelites mosied on down behind him.
Quiz 20—Think: Boone, Defoe, or Webster.
Quiz 21—Is that before or after we've been shorn?
Quiz 22—Some popular Caribbean islands share a word in this answer.
Quiz 23—It would be baaaaaaad if you missed this one.
Quiz 24—You can walk on it, too—if it's frozen.
Quiz 25—White or wheat?
Quiz 26—Surely a slithering, sneaky sort.
Quiz 27—Yes, you clean your sweaters with this.
Quiz 28—You might have swept the raw materials under your rug.
Quiz 29—Michael Jordan and Captain Picard make it easy for God...
Quiz 30—It was not barbecued.

Have a Hint

Level 2

Quiz 1—He later was his own judge and jury.
Quiz 2—It might begin, "Because..."
Quiz 3—You might find his name on your luggage.
Quiz 4—God is there when life gets woolly.
Quiz 5—In heaven, our most valuable stuff is pavement.
Quiz 6—Wood you like to take a guess?
Quiz 7—These critters aren't sacred.
Quiz 8—He shares a name with one of the Brady kids.
Quiz 9—John Steinbeck wrote of being "East of" there.
Quiz 10—No one gets left out...
Quiz 11—The "pot of gold" tradition came much later.
Quiz 12—So long and good-bye.
Quiz 13—It's "blue" in a classical waltz.
Quiz 14—Consider this: it fires a stone.
Quiz 15—They couldn't hold up their execution.
Quiz 16—At first, she seemed delightful.
Quiz 17—Add "Lee" for a dessert maker.
Quiz 18—Direct from God's kitchen...
Quiz 19—Mr. and Mrs., side by side.
Quiz 20—Hear that rumble? It's the sound of stomachs growling.
Quiz 21—As a talker, maybe he had the "gift of ___."
Quiz 22—Put that in a shaker!
Quiz 23—Like mild-mannered reporter Clark Kent...
Quiz 24—Why not start at the start?
Quiz 25—How's your knowledge of spirituals? "Joshua fit the battle of...."
Quiz 26—Animate, vital.
Quiz 27—They might be a girl's best friend, but the wise men weren't impressed.
Quiz 28—Built to last...
Quiz 29—Left to the imagination...
Quiz 30—Think: sweet and innocent.

Have a Hint

Level 3

Quiz 1—It was death, not laziness.
Quiz 2—That river had a lot of momentum.
Quiz 3—Think: chore.
Quiz 4—Like going from Don to Ron.
Quiz 5—Twelve-inch measurements. . .
Quiz 6—Pssst. . .I've got a secret!
Quiz 7—Arborvitae? Rhododendron? Rose?
Quiz 8—Think: baseball's "Hammerin' Hank."
Quiz 9—There's a type of apple with this name.
Quiz 10—Rivers and financial institutions have them.
Quiz 11—You'll typically notice it early in the morning.
Quiz 12—Think: hotel room Bibles.
Quiz 13—He has a farm building in his name.
Quiz 14—Easy, now. . .
Quiz 15—Joyful enthusiasm accompanied their birth.
Quiz 16—May I have a ____with you?
Quiz 17—It's not a request.
Quiz 18—We all have them on our legs.
Quiz 19—There are "American" and "French Foreign" versions.
Quiz 20—Add "angelo," and you've got a classical painter.
Quiz 21 It can go with "plow" or "ball."
Quiz 22—Some grow coconuts.
Quiz 23—Guardian angels. . .
Quiz 24—Add "oon" for a whaling spear.
Quiz 25—His friend had just died.
Quiz 26—American slaves liked to quote this verse.
Quiz 27—Your very heartbeat. . .
Quiz 28—An Irish million?
Quiz 29—The intimacy made the betrayal especially painful.
Quiz 30—It wasn't the size of the offering—it was the percentage.

Have a Hint

Bronze

Quiz 1—That sin is very serious stuff.
Quiz 2—Despite the sound of his name, he never flew an airplane.
Quiz 3—He also wrote the fourth Gospel.
Quiz 4—Troublemakers "raise" him.
Quiz 5—They're sweet, tender, and good for you.
Quiz 6—Remember, we're dealing with character qualities.
Quiz 7—Think: Barbie's boyfriend.
Quiz 8—Since there's no more death, it's...
Quiz 9—It sounds like confused chatter.
Quiz 10—He shares a name with a cactus the size of a tree.
Quiz 11—On an altar...
Quiz 12—A new kind of angler.
Quiz 13—Remember that God is a jealous God.
Quiz 14—Some say bad things come in threes.
Quiz 15—Like the Tour de France.
Quiz 16—It was a pretty smart request.
Quiz 17—Hymn title: "______Is the Victory."
Quiz 18—Mission accomplished.
Quiz 19—Like Fanny Crosby or Stevie Wonder.
Quiz 20—God would take him down, shake him up, make him new.
Quiz 21—He was not a popular guy.
Quiz 22—Those aren't squeals of delight...
Quiz 23—Add an "e" for a Christmas decoration.
Quiz 24—But not from Hershey's.
Quiz 25—French's or Grey Poupon might be interested.
Quiz 26—You might "say" it before dinner.
Quiz 27—Like Louis XVI and Marie Antoinette.
Quiz 28—As opposed to loss...
Quiz 29—He saw no value in the birthright.
Quiz 30—Where you'll find Beirut today.

HAVE A HINT

LEVEL 5

Quiz 1—Ironically, he first saw her bathing.
Quiz 2—It'll sneak up on you.
Quiz 3—Talk about a tight fit!
Quiz 4—"Doubting" is part of his name.
Quiz 5—He was at the end of his rope…
Quiz 6—Sounds like a chest-beating jungle hero…
Quiz 7—Think: "Jesus of ________."
Quiz 8—A special place…
Quiz 9—Shout "_____, hallelujah!"
Quiz 10—Belief in the unseen.
Quiz 11—Shares a name with a peninsula.
Quiz 12—Key word in question: "visiting."
Quiz 13—An unusual paint job…
Quiz 14—The Beatles said it's all you need.
Quiz 15—Zoos have them, too.
Quiz 16—Think: TV sitcom island…
Quiz 17—It cuts both ways.
Quiz 18—The third person of the Trinity.
Quiz 19—A mark of a merry person.
Quiz 20—Lowing and bleating.
Quiz 21—Like a church…
Quiz 22—Beating the doors down…
Quiz 23—Jesus called him a "rock"—like cement?
Quiz 24—Think: nomadic.
Quiz 25—Hold a picnic and he'll come to you…
Quiz 26—Like she'd just heard a punch line…
Quiz 27—Think: DiMaggio or Stalin.
Quiz 28—The square root of 49.
Quiz 29—His name goes with "ladder."
Quiz 30—He was horrid…

Have a Hint

Level 6

Quiz 1—Grief, anguish, woe.
Quiz 2—Think: Asimov or Bashevis Singer.
Quiz 3—Cupidity, avarice, greed.
Quiz 4—With a smile!
Quiz 5—Shazaam—a talking donkey?
Quiz 6—The first shall be last.
Quiz 7—Like riding a spiritual elevator…
Quiz 8—Slightly over 16 percent.
Quiz 9—You should do this before dinner, too.
Quiz 10—Jesus is always the best example.
Quiz 11—Not all advice is good advice.
Quiz 12—Comprehension.
Quiz 13—His eye is on it.
Quiz 14—One-ninth of a year!
Quiz 15—We're talking lots (and lots) of wives.
Quiz 16—Probably the least impressive way…
Quiz 17—Filet mignon, anyone?
Quiz 18—He shares a name with another key Bible character.
Quiz 19—Think: five-sided things.
Quiz 20—A symbol of peace.
Quiz 21—Before you're long in the tooth…
Quiz 22—Yen to pounds to francs, etc.
Quiz 23—Think: constrictorz.
Quiz 24—Bo Peep's among Big Bads.
Quiz 25—Like William the…
Quiz 26—Also known as leaven.
Quiz 27—Think: Lincoln's opponent Douglas.
Quiz 28—Carter and Kennedy…
Quiz 29—A sort of alchemy?
Quiz 30—A symbol of peace.

Have a Hint

Level 7

Quiz 1—A man's home is his embassy.
Quiz 2—Mind your manners: Say ______.
Quiz 3—Sounds like a PLO leader.
Quiz 4—Think: Big diamond at the Smithsonian...
Quiz 5—It's the only one who shares a name with a biblical book.
Quiz 6—The King James might say, "A man diest."
Quiz 7—Like Androcles's lion friend.
Quiz 8—Knock, knock. Who's there?
Quiz 9—Atheists, et al.
Quiz 10—Judas had tried to return the money, in vein.
Quiz 11—Is it getting hot in here?
Quiz 12—United in spirit...and body.
Quiz 13—It was his major claim to fame.
Quiz 14—He was the disciples' treasurer...
Quiz 15—Quite an irony, actually.
Quiz 16—And perhaps his tight stomach muscles...
Quiz 17—Heads up!
Quiz 18—Think: "penny."
Quiz 19—In present-day Syria.
Quiz 20—An F-4 or F-5, perhaps?
Quiz 21—He's pretty bright...
Quiz 22—Don't blame the blameless.
Quiz 23—Where not even the *Red October* could find them.
Quiz 24—"______ can you see, by the dawn's early light?"
Quiz 25—One for each dime in a dollar.
Quiz 26—For those pyramids, perhaps?
Quiz 27—This love covered a multitude of sins.
Quiz 28—Think: Moammar Kadaffi's country...
Quiz 29—Just do it.
Quiz 30—He shares a name with *Moby Dick*'s narrator.

Have a Hint

Silver

Quiz 1—And never the two shall meet...
Quiz 2—He's a king, all right.
Quiz 3—Jesus saw right through the temptation...
Quiz 4—Think: indent key.
Quiz 5—It's more than an emotion.
Quiz 6—But nobody wrote a biblical book to them.
Quiz 7—First person, present tense.
Quiz 8—Think: ice cream and root beer...
Quiz 9—Think: Diller or Schlafly.
Quiz 10—I can't get no satisfaction...
Quiz 11—Say what?
Quiz 12—Let's ask Bill Gates.
Quiz 13—Think: President Jackson.
Quiz 14—As pie, so they say.
Quiz 15—The final and most serious...
Quiz 16—Legionnaires.
Quiz 17—"I am the light of the world."
Quiz 18—Today, he'd use Velcro.
Quiz 19—Economists call it a labor shortage.
Quiz 20—Censure or blame.
Quiz 21—Modern proverbs say laughter is the best medicine.
Quiz 22—No chariots of fire this time.
Quiz 23—John was a rough, outdoorsy type.
Quiz 24—Strumpet, harlot.
Quiz 25—Shares a name with the Dickens' character Heep.
Quiz 26—Shortly before humans, who were last.
Quiz 27—Shares a name with U.S. patriot Hale.
Quiz 28—But not the kind that makes you scream.
Quiz 29—Sounds like a place for recovering alcoholics...
Quiz 30—Think: Pat Boone's daughter.

Have a Hint

Level 9

Quiz 1—Philadelphia is the City of...
Quiz 2—Perhaps named after an Old Testament forefather?
Quiz 3—A real word picture.
Quiz 4—America's favorite uncle...
Quiz 5—If you can pronounce it, move to the head of the class.
Quiz 6—Like Heber's famous hymn.
Quiz 7—Abel's death...
Quiz 8—At nine in the morning?
Quiz 9—He made a mockery of the gift of grace.
Quiz 10—It follows the Song of Solomon.
Quiz 11—Gobletman.
Quiz 12—Add an "e" for a man's name.
Quiz 13—But they didn't wear jeans when they worked.
Quiz 14—With his closest associates...
Quiz 15—One of Ben Franklin's two certainties...
Quiz 16—Sometimes it's forked.
Quiz 17—There's a Jane Austen title in the name.
Quiz 18—Chicago had a big one in 1871.
Quiz 19—Think: "____ Karenina."
Quiz 20—Cain followed in his footsteps.
Quiz 21—A cartoon character from Yosemite shares his name.
Quiz 22—It can't buy you love, either.
Quiz 23—Big fish for ________.
Quiz 24—It predated the Richter Scale.
Quiz 25—He took a brief walk on the wet side.
Quiz 26—It's not really "against" anything...
Quiz 27—Where you'd sometimes find a hook.
Quiz 28—The sons of Zebedee.
Quiz 29—They wanted to keep a good man down...
Quiz 30—More than the miles of Indianapolis...

Have a Hint

Level 10

Quiz 1—Think: the study of God.
Quiz 2—No spelunking required.
Quiz 3—A biblical author...
Quiz 4—He shared a name with Peter.
Quiz 5—There's a fishing pole in his name.
Quiz 6—Add an "ng" to determine who did him in.
Quiz 7—Like a firm parent with a picky child...
Quiz 8—A real difficulty for Copernicus.
Quiz 9—Pup or circus?
Quiz 10—He's generally known as the most aggressive, anyway.
Quiz 11—A city that would later host the first modern Olympics.
Quiz 12—Mobile meals?
Quiz 13—Think: a modern musical genre.
Quiz 14—Perhaps from the Napa Valley?
Quiz 15—No man can serve two masters...
Quiz 16—Sounds like the famous quarterback "Broadway Joe."
Quiz 17—Figuratively, it's good luck for an actor.
Quiz 18—A day for each year of the Israelites' wilderness wanderings.
Quiz 19—Think: 700 Club's Robertson.
Quiz 20—Agricultural instruments.
Quiz 21—What more could God ask?
Quiz 22—Avoid alliterating appellations...
Quiz 23—Like someone dialing 911.
Quiz 24—Gimme another...
Quiz 25—Did people want to "be like" him?
Quiz 26—Shares a name with the novelist Hawthorne.
Quiz 27—Shares a name with a tribe of Israel.
Quiz 28—It's a relative thing...
Quiz 29—Think: bachelor.
Quiz 30—Think: baseball headwear.

Have a Hint

Level 11

Quiz 1—Sounds like partway to somewhere.
Quiz 2—He has a machine gun in his name.
Quiz 3—No work for the sandman.
Quiz 4—Add an "H" for an old-fashioned cheer.
Quiz 5—Think: street.
Quiz 6—He was too busy fighting off trials.
Quiz 7—She was pregnant for at least sixty-three months (total!).
Quiz 8—Sounds like a bumblebee...
Quiz 9—That's called "immunity"!
Quiz 10—He could have gotten death.
Quiz 11—He interpreted the "handwriting on the wall."
Quiz 12—It was his only claim to fame.
Quiz 13—Sounds like a bad grade in school...
Quiz 14—Normally, that would hurt!
Quiz 15—The same guy who had anointed him king...
Quiz 16—Jesus said to him, "Feed my sheep."
Quiz 17—Supposedly, they "are forever."
Quiz 18—He just missed the millenary.
Quiz 19—This name has a "ring" to it.
Quiz 20—The first queen had acted rashly.
Quiz 21—If you can't say something nice, don't say anything at all.
Quiz 22—His rods and cones weren't working.
Quiz 23—A promise—and a warning?
Quiz 24—He had had a personal sermon on being "born again."
Quiz 25—It's all we know about this person.
Quiz 26—Take a number...
Quiz 27—He was feeling like his name...
Quiz 28—They say it's a crowd...
Quiz 29—How would they keep the doctors away?
Quiz 30—A 60s song said he was a bullfrog...

Have a Hint

Gold

Quiz 1—Today he's a well-known cookie maker.
Quiz 2—Jesus said it was neither hot nor cold—though there's something freezing in its name.
Quiz 3—Sounds like: _______-Seltzer.
Quiz 4—...by the Fourth of July–ah.
Quiz 5—They just don't have a ring to them.
Quiz 6—He sounds like a third-place kind of guy (primary, secondary...).
Quiz 7—No STP needed.
Quiz 8—I'd be really pleased if you could guess this!
Quiz 9—Puff, the Magic...?
Quiz 10—You're toast!
Quiz 11—That's a pretty fair family.
Quiz 12—Just outside the promised land.
Quiz 13—Its days were "numbered."
Quiz 14—This name came in twos, too.
Quiz 15—MGM would be disappointed.
Quiz 16—When their mother called them "big boys," she meant it.
Quiz 17—Did you muster an answer?
Quiz 18—Think: white sphere on a pool table.
Quiz 19—What do you have when sitting that you don't have when standing?
Quiz 20—Were there snakes there?
Quiz 21—Think: Sears, Trump, CN.
Quiz 22—Paul's "bachelor pad."
Quiz 23—Eight years old? No joke.
Quiz 24—What if that happened to you?
Quiz 25—What would Freud have thought?
Quiz 26—If you get this, you're pretty smart!
Quiz 27—People loved to be around him.
Quiz 28—He might have occasionally gotten the tax collector's mail...
Quiz 29—Think: Confederate president.
Quiz 30—To show the straight and true...

Look in the Book

Level 1

Quiz 1—Genesis 2:20
Quiz 2—Genesis 7:1–2
Quiz 3—1 Samuel 17:4, 50
Quiz 4—Matthew 1:16
Quiz 5—Exodus 20:1–21
Quiz 6—Genesis 3:20
Quiz 7—Jonah 1:17
Quiz 8—Genesis 17:5
Quiz 9—Luke 6:13–16
Quiz 10—Daniel 3
Quiz 11—Genesis 2:2
Quiz 12—Luke 6:13
Quiz 13—Luke 19:2–4
Quiz 14—Luke 10:29–37
Quiz 15—Genesis 37:3
Quiz 16—Luke 2:4–6
Quiz 17—Matthew 2:9
Quiz 18—Luke 2:16
Quiz 19—Exodus 6:13
Quiz 20—Daniel 6
Quiz 21—John 10:14
Quiz 22—Matthew 1:23
Quiz 23—John 10:14
Quiz 24—John 6:19
Quiz 25—John 6:35
Quiz 26—Genesis 3:1–6
Quiz 27—Joshua 24:11
Quiz 28—Genesis 2:7
Quiz 29—Matthew 10:30
Quiz 30—Genesis 2:21

Look in the Book

Level 2

Quiz 1—Matthew 26:14–15
Quiz 2—John 3:16
Quiz 3—Judges 16:6, 17
Quiz 4—Psalm 23:1
Quiz 5—Revelation 21:21
Quiz 6—Matthew 13:55
Quiz 7—Psalm 50:10
Quiz 8—Matthew 26:75
Quiz 9—Genesis 2:8
Quiz 10—Romans 3:23
Quiz 11—Genesis 9:16
Quiz 12—Genesis 19:24
Quiz 13—Genesis 2:10–14
Quiz 14—1 Samuel 17:48–49
Quiz 15—Matthew 27:38
Quiz 16—Judges 16:18
Quiz 17—Genesis 17:15
Quiz 18—Exodus 16:31
Quiz 19—Genesis 7:8–9
Quiz 20—Genesis 41:25–28
Quiz 21—Luke 1:26–27
Quiz 22—Genesis 19:26
Quiz 23—Matthew 5:5
Quiz 24—Genesis 1:1
Quiz 25—Joshua 6:1, 20
Quiz 26—John 4:10
Quiz 27—Matthew 2:11
Quiz 28—Exodus 31:18
Quiz 29—Genesis 3:6
Quiz 30—John 1:29

Look in the Book

Level 3

Quiz 1—John 11:43–44
Quiz 2—Exodus 2:1–10
Quiz 3—Job 3:1
Quiz 4—Acts 13:9
Quiz 5—Psalm 119:105
Quiz 6—Exodus 20:3–17
Quiz 7—Exodus 3:2–10
Quiz 8—Exodus 7:1
Quiz 9—1 Samuel 18:1
Quiz 10—John 15:5
Quiz 11—John 18:27
Quiz 12—Judges 6:36–37
Quiz 13—Acts 13:2
Quiz 14—Ezekiel 1:2–16
Quiz 15—Genesis 25:24–26
Quiz 16—John 1:1
Quiz 17—Matthew 6:9
Quiz 18—Exodus 32:4
Quiz 19—Mark 5:9
Quiz 20—Jude 9
Quiz 21—Psalm 51:7
Quiz 22—John 12:13
Quiz 23—Genesis 3:24
Quiz 24—1 Samuel 16:23
Quiz 25—John 11:35
Quiz 26—John 8:32
Quiz 27—John 14:6
Quiz 28—Revelation 22:13
Quiz 29—Matthew 26:48
Quiz 30—Luke 21:2–3

Look in the Book

Bronze

Quiz 1—Romans 6:23
Quiz 2—John 19:16
Quiz 3—Revelation 1:9–11
Quiz 4—Genesis 4:8
Quiz 5—Galatians 5:22–23
Quiz 6—Galatians 5:22–23
Quiz 7—Genesis 9:18
Quiz 8—Revelation 21:27
Quiz 9—Genesis 11:9
Quiz 10—Numbers 27:22–23
Quiz 11—Genesis 22:2
Quiz 12—Matthew 4:19
Quiz 13—Exodus 20:3
Quiz 14—Revelation 13:18
Quiz 15—2 Timothy 4:7
Quiz 16—2 Chronicles 1:10
Quiz 17—Romans 1:17
Quiz 18—John 19:30
Quiz 19—Acts 9:9
Quiz 20—Genesis 32:24–28
Quiz 21—Matthew 9:9
Quiz 22—Mark 5:12–13
Quiz 23—Proverbs 15:1
Quiz 24—1 Thessalonians 5:26
Quiz 25—Luke 13:18–19
Quiz 26—Ephesians 2:8
Quiz 27—Matthew 14:10
Quiz 28—Philippians 1:21
Quiz 29—Genesis 25:34
Quiz 30—1 Kings 5:8–9

Look in the Book

Level 5

Quiz 1—2 Samuel 11:2–3
Quiz 2—1Thessalonians 5:2
Quiz 3—Mark 10:25
Quiz 4—John 20:24–25
Quiz 5—Matthew 27:5
Quiz 6—Acts 9:11
Quiz 7—Luke 4:16
Quiz 8—Matthew 5:3
Quiz 9—Psalm 19:1
Quiz 10—Ephesians 6:16
Quiz 11—Exodus 19:20
Quiz 12—1 Kings 10:4–7
Quiz 13—Exodus 12:7, 13
Quiz 14—1 John 4:8
Quiz 15—Genesis 4:9
Quiz 16—Jeremiah 8:22
Quiz 17—Hebrews 4:12
Quiz 18—Romans 8:26
Quiz 19—1 Corinthians 15:52
Quiz 20—1 Samuel 15:13–14
Quiz 21—1 Corinthians 6:19
Quiz 22—Matthew 16:18
Quiz 23—John 1:42
Quiz 24—Luke 9:58
Quiz 25—Proverbs 6:6
Quiz 26—Genesis 18:12
Quiz 27—Genesis 39:4–7
Quiz 28—Revelation 1:20
Quiz 29—Genesis 32:28
Quiz 30—Matthew 2:16

Look in the Book

Level 6

Quiz 1—Isaiah 53:3
Quiz 2—Genesis 25:26
Quiz 3—1 Timothy 6:10
Quiz 4—2 Corinthians 9:7
Quiz 5—Numbers 22:21, 28
Quiz 6—Matthew 23:11
Quiz 7—2 Kings 2:1
Quiz 8—Numbers 14:6–7
Quiz 9—Matthew 27:24
Quiz 10—Ephesians 5:25
Quiz 11—Job 2:9
Quiz 12—Proverbs 3:5
Quiz 13—Matthew 10:29
Quiz 14—Matthew 4:2
Quiz 15—1 Kings 11:3
Quiz 16—Matthew 21:7
Quiz 17—Leviticus 11:3–8
Quiz 18—Matthew 3:1–3
Quiz 19—Acts 2:1–4
Quiz 20—Genesis 8:11
Quiz 21—Ecclesiastes 12:1
Quiz 22—Mark 11:15
Quiz 23—Ruth 4:13
Quiz 24—Matthew 10:16
Quiz 25—Romans 8:37
Quiz 26—Matthew 13:33
Quiz 27—Acts 7:54–60
Quiz 28—Mark 10:35–37
Quiz 29—John 2:9–11
Quiz 30—Luke 3:22

Look in the Book

Level 7

Quiz 1—2 Corinthians 5:20
Quiz 2—Philippians 4:8
Quiz 3—Genesis 8:4
Quiz 4—Isaiah 9:6
Quiz 5—Esther 2:7
Quiz 6—Acts 5:1–11
Quiz 7—2 Corinthians 12:7
Quiz 8—Genesis 5:24
Quiz 9—2 Corinthians 6:14
Quiz 10—Matthew 27:7–8
Quiz 11—1 Corinthians 7:9
Quiz 12—Genesis 2:24
Quiz 13—Genesis 5:27
Quiz 14—John 12:6
Quiz 15—John 19:19
Quiz 16—2 Samuel 14:25
Quiz 17—Colossians 3:2
Quiz 18—Matthew 8:5–13
Quiz 19—Acts 9:3
Quiz 20—Acts 2:2
Quiz 21—2 Corinthians 11:14
Quiz 22—James 1:13
Quiz 23—Micah 7:19
Quiz 24—Hosea 1:2
Quiz 25—Genesis 18:32
Quiz 26—Exodus 5:7
Quiz 27—Romans 5:8
Quiz 28—Acts 16:14
Quiz 29—James 2:20
Quiz 30—Genesis 16:15

Look in the Book

Silver

Quiz 1—Psalm 103:12
Quiz 2—Isaiah 38:5
Quiz 3—Matthew 4:1–10
Quiz 4—Acts 9:40
Quiz 5—1 Corinthians 13:8
Quiz 6—Acts 17:10–11
Quiz 7—Exodus 3:14
Quiz 8—2 Kings 6:6
Quiz 9—1 Samuel 17:4
Quiz 10—1 Timothy 6:6
Quiz 11—James 3:8
Quiz 12—Proverbs 22:1
Quiz 13—Mark 14:32–33
Quiz 14—Matthew 11:30
Quiz 15—Revelation 6:1–8
Quiz 16—John 19:2
Quiz 17—John 8:12
Quiz 18—Luke 3:16
Quiz 19—Matthew 9:37
Quiz 20—Romans 8:1
Quiz 21—Proverbs 17:22
Quiz 22—1 Thessalonians 4:16
Quiz 23—Matthew 3:4
Quiz 24—Revelation 17:1–3
Quiz 25—2 Samuel 11:3, 15
Quiz 26—Genesis 1:20–23
Quiz 27—2 Samuel 12:7
Quiz 28—Psalm 111:10
Quiz 29—Hebrews 11:31
Quiz 30—Judges 4:4, 24

Look in the Book

Level 9

Quiz 1—John 13:35
Quiz 2—Mark 15:43
Quiz 3—Matthew 27:33
Quiz 4—Luke 9:30–31
Quiz 5—Hebrews 5:6
Quiz 6—Isaiah 6:3
Quiz 7—Genesis 4:25
Quiz 8—Acts 2:13
Quiz 9—Acts 8:20
Quiz 10—Acts 8:30
Quiz 11—Nehemiah 1:11
Quiz 12—1 Samuel 18:27
Quiz 13—Numbers 1:50–51
Quiz 14—Mark 6:4
Quiz 15—Luke 20:21–25
Quiz 16—Proverbs 18:21
Quiz 17—Luke 24:13–16
Quiz 18—Matthew 13:44, 47; 22:2
Quiz 19—Matthew 21:9
Quiz 20—John 8:44
Quiz 21—1 Samuel 1:19–20
Quiz 22—Proverbs 11:4
Quiz 23—Jonah 1:3
Quiz 24—Matthew 27:51, 28:2
Quiz 25—Mark 1:30–31
Quiz 26—Acts 11:26
Quiz 27—Matthew 17:27
Quiz 28—Mark 3:17
Quiz 29—John 12:10
Quiz 30—1 Corinthians 15:6

Look in the Book

Level 10

Quiz 1—Acts 1:1
Quiz 2—Daniel 4:33
Quiz 3—Acts 15:37–38
Quiz 4—Mark 15:21
Quiz 5—Genesis 10:9
Quiz 6—Esther 7:10
Quiz 7—2 Thessalonians 3:10
Quiz 8—Joshua 10:13
Quiz 9—Acts 18:3
Quiz 10—John 20:4–6
Quiz 11—Acts 17: 22–23
Quiz 12—Acts 10:9–28
Quiz 13—Daniel 2:32–34
Quiz 14—1 Timothy 5:23
Quiz 15—James 4:4
Quiz 16—2 Kings 5:11
Quiz 17—John 19:32
Quiz 18—Acts 1:3
Quiz 19—Revelation 1:9
Quiz 20—Isaiah 2:4
Quiz 21—Genesis 22:2
Quiz 22—Job 2:11
Quiz 23—Acts 16:9–10
Quiz 24—2 Kings 2:9
Quiz 25—Micah 5:2
Quiz 26—John 1:46
Quiz 27—Luke 2:21–35
Quiz 28—Esther 9:31
Quiz 29—1 Corinthians 7:7–8
Quiz 30—Matthew 4:13

Look in the Book

Level 11

Quiz 1—Exodus 2:15
Quiz 2—Isaiah 6:1–8
Quiz 3—Ecclesiastes 3:1–8
Quiz 4—2 Samuel 6:6–7
Quiz 5—Acts 12:13
Quiz 6—Proverbs 1:1, 30:1, 31:1
Quiz 7—Mark 6:3
Quiz 8—Job 1:1
Quiz 9—Acts 28:1–6
Quiz 10—2 Samuel 9:13
Quiz 11—Daniel 1:7
Quiz 12—Acts 23:12–16
Quiz 13—Acts 19:23–34
Quiz 14—Isaiah 6:6–7
Quiz 15—1 Samuel 28:11
Quiz 16—Acts 5:15
Quiz 17—Revelation 21:19–20
Quiz 18—Genesis 5:27
Quiz 19—Daniel 5
Quiz 20—Esther 2:17
Quiz 21—2 Kings 2:23–24
Quiz 22—Mark 10:46, 52
Quiz 23—Revelation 22:20
Quiz 24—John 19:39
Quiz 25—Luke 24:18
Quiz 26—1 Chronicles 21:1, 14
Quiz 27—Joshua 7:20–25
Quiz 28—2 Corinthians 11:25
Quiz 29—Numbers 11:5
Quiz 30—Jeremiah 38:4–6

Look in the Book

Gold

Quiz 1—Amos 1:1
Quiz 2—Revelation 3:14–16
Quiz 3—John 18:10
Quiz 4—Nehemiah 6:1–2
Quiz 5—Song of Solomon 7:1–5
Quiz 6—Romans 16:22
Quiz 7—Proverbs 5:3
Quiz 8—Job 9:9
Quiz 9—1 Samuel 5:4
Quiz 10—Proverbs 6:26
Quiz 11—Judges 10:3–4
Quiz 12—Jude 9
Quiz 13—Nahum 1:1
Quiz 14—Numbers 27:1
Quiz 15—Nehemiah 3:13–15
Quiz 16—1 Chronicles 20:5
Quiz 17—John 20:24
Quiz 18—Genesis 4:21
Quiz 19—Judges 4:4
Quiz 20—2 Samuel 1:6–10
Quiz 21—Luke 13:4–5
Quiz 22—Acts 28:30
Quiz 23—2 Kings 22:1, 23:25
Quiz 24—Acts 20:9
Quiz 25—Matthew 27:19
Quiz 26—2 Samuel 12:24–25
Quiz 27—Acts 4:36
Quiz 28—Acts 1:26
Quiz 29—Judges 11:30–40
Quiz 30—Amos 7:8

Answers

Level 1

Quiz 1—B
Quiz 2—C
Quiz 3—A
Quiz 4—D
Quiz 5—C
Quiz 6—A
Quiz 7—C
Quiz 8—A
Quiz 9—C
Quiz 10—B
Quiz 11—D
Quiz 12—B
Quiz 13—A
Quiz 14—C
Quiz 15—B
Quiz 16—A
Quiz 17—D
Quiz 18—C
Quiz 19—C
Quiz 20—B
Quiz 21—C
Quiz 22—C
Quiz 23—B
Quiz 24—A
Quiz 25—D
Quiz 26—C
Quiz 27—D
Quiz 28—C
Quiz 29—A
Quiz 30—B

Answers

Level 2

Quiz 1—C
Quiz 2—D
Quiz 3—B
Quiz 4—B
Quiz 5—A
Quiz 6—C
Quiz 7—B
Quiz 8—D
Quiz 9—A
Quiz 10—D
Quiz 11—A
Quiz 12—C
Quiz 13—D
Quiz 14—C
Quiz 15—B
Quiz 16—C
Quiz 17—B
Quiz 18—C
Quiz 19—B
Quiz 20—A
Quiz 21—C
Quiz 22—D
Quiz 23—D
Quiz 24—C
Quiz 25—A
Quiz 26—A
Quiz 27—B
Quiz 28—C
Quiz 29—D
Quiz 30—D

Answers

Level 3

Quiz 1—A
Quiz 2—B
Quiz 3—C
Quiz 4—C
Quiz 5—A
Quiz 6—D
Quiz 7—B
Quiz 8—C
Quiz 9—D
Quiz 10—C
Quiz 11—D
Quiz 12—B
Quiz 13—A
Quiz 14—A
Quiz 15—B
Quiz 16—D
Quiz 17—C
Quiz 18—A
Quiz 19—B
Quiz 20—A
Quiz 21—B
Quiz 22—C
Quiz 23—C
Quiz 24—B
Quiz 25—B
Quiz 26—A
Quiz 27—A
Quiz 28—C
Quiz 29—A
Quiz 30—D

Answers

Bronze

Quiz 1—C
Quiz 2—B
Quiz 3—A
Quiz 4—B
Quiz 5—C
Quiz 6—B
Quiz 7—C
Quiz 8—B
Quiz 9—A
Quiz 10—B
Quiz 11—A
Quiz 12—D
Quiz 13—C
Quiz 14—C
Quiz 15—B
Quiz 16—C
Quiz 17—A
Quiz 18—C
Quiz 19—D
Quiz 20—C
Quiz 21—D
Quiz 22—B
Quiz 23—A
Quiz 24—B
Quiz 25—C
Quiz 26—B
Quiz 27—B
Quiz 28—A
Quiz 29—D
Quiz 30—A

Answers

Level 5

Quiz 1—A
Quiz 2—A
Quiz 3—B
Quiz 4—D
Quiz 5—A
Quiz 6—C
Quiz 7—B
Quiz 8—B
Quiz 9—A
Quiz 10—C
Quiz 11—D
Quiz 12—A
Quiz 13—D
Quiz 14—B
Quiz 15—D
Quiz 16—C
Quiz 17—B
Quiz 18—D
Quiz 19—A
Quiz 20—B
Quiz 21—A
Quiz 22—C
Quiz 23—B
Quiz 24—C
Quiz 25—D
Quiz 26—A
Quiz 27—D
Quiz 28—C
Quiz 29—C
Quiz 30—D

Answers

Level 6

Quiz 1—B
Quiz 2—C
Quiz 3—D
Quiz 4—A
Quiz 5—D
Quiz 6—D
Quiz 7—A
Quiz 8—C
Quiz 9—D
Quiz 10—B
Quiz 11—C
Quiz 12—B
Quiz 13—A
Quiz 14—D
Quiz 15—D
Quiz 16—C
Quiz 17—C
Quiz 18—A
Quiz 19—B
Quiz 20—D
Quiz 21—A
Quiz 22—C
Quiz 23—B
Quiz 24—B
Quiz 25—A
Quiz 26—D
Quiz 27—A
Quiz 28—A
Quiz 29—D
Quiz 30—B

Answers

Level 7

Quiz 1—C
Quiz 2—D
Quiz 3—A
Quiz 4—D
Quiz 5—B
Quiz 6—C
Quiz 7—A
Quiz 8—B
Quiz 9—B
Quiz 10—A
Quiz 11—C
Quiz 12—A
Quiz 13—C
Quiz 14—C
Quiz 15—B
Quiz 16—B
Quiz 17—A
Quiz 18—A
Quiz 19—D
Quiz 20—B
Quiz 21—C
Quiz 22—D
Quiz 23—C
Quiz 24—B
Quiz 25—D
Quiz 26—C
Quiz 27—B
Quiz 28—A
Quiz 29—D
Quiz 30—A

Answers

Silver

Quiz 1—A
Quiz 2—B
Quiz 3—D
Quiz 4—A
Quiz 5—A
Quiz 6—B
Quiz 7—C
Quiz 8—C
Quiz 9—A
Quiz 10—C
Quiz 11—D
Quiz 12—A
Quiz 13—A
Quiz 14—C
Quiz 15—B
Quiz 16—D
Quiz 17—C
Quiz 18—B
Quiz 19—B
Quiz 20—A
Quiz 21—C
Quiz 22—B
Quiz 23—D
Quiz 24—C
Quiz 25—A
Quiz 26—D
Quiz 27—C
Quiz 28—C
Quiz 29—B
Quiz 30—B

Answers

Level 9

Quiz 1—C
Quiz 2—B
Quiz 3—C
Quiz 4—D
Quiz 5—D
Quiz 6—A
Quiz 7—A
Quiz 8—C
Quiz 9—D
Quiz 10—C
Quiz 11—C
Quiz 12—A
Quiz 13—C
Quiz 14—B
Quiz 15—C
Quiz 16—A
Quiz 17—A
Quiz 18—C
Quiz 19—A
Quiz 20—D
Quiz 21—B
Quiz 22—B
Quiz 23—D
Quiz 24—C
Quiz 25—B
Quiz 26—A
Quiz 27—B
Quiz 28—C
Quiz 29—C
Quiz 30—D

Answers

Level 10

Quiz 1—A
Quiz 2—D
Quiz 3—B
Quiz 4—B
Quiz 5—C
Quiz 6—C
Quiz 7—B
Quiz 8—D
Quiz 9—C
Quiz 10—B
Quiz 11—A
Quiz 12—C
Quiz 13—D
Quiz 14—A
Quiz 15—B
Quiz 16—C
Quiz 17—D
Quiz 18—C
Quiz 19—B
Quiz 20—A
Quiz 21—D
Quiz 22—D
Quiz 23—B
Quiz 24—A
Quiz 25—C
Quiz 26—D
Quiz 27—B
Quiz 28—A
Quiz 29—D
Quiz 30—A

Answers

Level 11

Quiz 1—D
Quiz 2—B
Quiz 3—B
Quiz 4—A
Quiz 5—C
Quiz 6—A
Quiz 7—D
Quiz 8—A
Quiz 9—B
Quiz 10—D
Quiz 11—B
Quiz 12—A
Quiz 13—A
Quiz 14—C
Quiz 15—D
Quiz 16—C
Quiz 17—A
Quiz 18—C
Quiz 19—C
Quiz 20—A
Quiz 21—D
Quiz 22—C
Quiz 23—C
Quiz 24—D
Quiz 25—D
Quiz 26—C
Quiz 27—A
Quiz 28—C
Quiz 29—D
Quiz 30—C

Answers

Gold

Quiz 1—C
Quiz 2—D
Quiz 3—A
Quiz 4—B
Quiz 5—C
Quiz 6—C
Quiz 7—A
Quiz 8—B
Quiz 9—A
Quiz 10—D
Quiz 11—B
Quiz 12—D
Quiz 13—D
Quiz 14—D
Quiz 15—C
Quiz 16—B
Quiz 17—A
Quiz 18—B
Quiz 19—A
Quiz 20—D
Quiz 21—B
Quiz 22—D
Quiz 23—A
Quiz 24—A
Quiz 25—C
Quiz 26—B
Quiz 27—B
Quiz 28—C
Quiz 29—B
Quiz 30—D

MY FINAL ANSWER

CELEBRITY EDITION

THIRTY INTERACTIVE QUIZZES THAT PUT *YOU* IN THE HOT SEAT

JOHN HUDSON TINER

QUIZZES

THIRTY INTERACTIVE QUIZZES THAT PUT YOU IN THE HOT SEAT

TRIVIA FOR LIFE

Quiz 1

Level 1

What was the first major publication from Johannes Gutenberg's printing press?

a) *Poor Richard's Almanack*
b) Saint Augustine's book *The City of God*
c) the entire Bible
d) the Dead Sea Scrolls

Level 2

What letters did Joni Eareckson Tada use to sign her first paintings?

a) GIG for "God Is Good"
b) PTL for "Praise the Lord"
c) WWJD for "What Would Jesus Do?"
d) JAF for "Joni and Friends"

Pages 337–338 Pages 349–350 Pages 361–362 Pages 373–374

Level 3

In addition to Genesis, what other book of the Bible starts "In the beginning"?

a) Job
b) Daniel
c) Luke
d) John

Bronze

The phrase "Come, we that love the Lord" is from what song by Isaac Watts?

a) "I'm Not Ashamed to Own My Lord"
b) "Sing the Mighty Power of God"
c) "We're Marching to Zion"
d) "There Is a Land of Pure Delight"

Level 5

What was the blind man doing when he called to Jesus on the road outside Jericho?

a) begging
b) weaving fabric
c) resting
d) making pottery

Level 6

To escape from Herod, where did Joseph and Mary take Baby Jesus?

a) Ethiopia
b) Rome
c) Tyre
d) Egypt

Pages 339–342 Pages 351–354 Pages 363–366 Pages 375–378

Level 7

Which would best describe Dwight L. Moody's approach to his ministry?

a) conservative and personal Christianity
b) higher criticism of the Bible
c) promoting unity among Christian denominations
d) speaking effectively for the Social Gospel movement

Silver

Which of the following works is by the artist Albrecht Dürer?

a) *Hands of the Apostle,* better known as "praying hands"
b) *The Adoration of the Magi*
c) *Madonna and Child with the Infant St. John*
d) *Pietà* in St. Peter's Basilica

Level 9

What job did Rachel do?

a) shepherdess
b) seamstress
c) groomed horses
d) hired servant

Pages 343–345 Pages 355–357 Pages 367–369 Pages 379–381

LEVEL 10

George Macdonald, who influenced C. S. Lewis, wrote what children's book?

a) *At the Back of the North Wind*
b) *The Natural History of a Candle*
c) *The Swiss Family Robinson*
d) *The Secret Garden*

LEVEL 11

How many years older was Aaron than Moses?

a) three years
b) twenty years
c) twelve years
d) none, they were twins

GOLD

Who was the person who first wrapped Jesus' crucified body in about seventy-five pounds of myrrh and aloes?

a) Nicodemus
b) Joanna
c) Mary Magdalene and the "other" Mary
d) Martha

Pages 346–348 Pages 358–360 Pages 370–372 Pages 382–384

QUIZ 2

LEVEL 1

In the motto of his abolitionist paper, who did Frederick Douglass say was "father of us all"?

a) God
b) invention
c) truth
d) poverty

LEVEL 2

How did Mary describe herself to the angel who announced she would give birth to Jesus?

a) "[The Lord] has shown his favor and taken away my disgrace."
b) "I am the Lord's servant."
c) "Why is this happening to me?"
d) "I am worn out and my master is old."

Pages 337–338 Pages 349–350 Pages 361–362 Pages 373–374

Level 3

In his song, what time of day does Charles Austin Miles enter "In the Garden"?

a) "in the cool of the day"
b) "while the dew is still on the roses"
c) "though the night around me is falling"
d) "at three in the afternoon"

Bronze

What was Cain's reply when God asked him about his brother?

a) "Here am I."
b) "Am I my brother's keeper?"
c) "Am I in the place of God?"
d) "What wrong am I guilty of?"

Level 5

What was the profession of Lew Wallace, the author of *Ben-Hur*?

a) scientist
b) explorer
c) missionary
d) military leader

Level 6

Complete this quotation by George Washington Carver: "It is service to others that measures. . ." ?

a) "success."
b) "heavenly compensation."
c) "genius."
d) "achieved dreams."

Pages 339–342 Pages 351–354 Pages 363–366 Pages 375–378

Level 7

How is Tabitha described in the Bible?

a) as carrying gossip and sowing strife
b) as the first Christian in Europe
c) as a woman who had been sick for twelve years
d) as doing good and helping the poor

Silver

What type of water is described in "Jesus, Keep Me Near the Cross" by Fanny J. Crosby?

a) "an ocean deep"
b) "a healing stream"
c) "rain for a thirsty land"
d) "cool, melting snow"

Level 9

What was George Whitefield's greatest strength as a preacher?

a) his dignified presentation
b) his scholarship
c) his profound theological ideas
d) his dramatic speaking style

Pages 343–345 Pages 355–357 Pages 367–369 Pages 379–381

Level 10

How did Jesus reply when Martha said, "If you had been here my brother would not have died"?

a) "Your brother will rise again."
b) "Don't be alarmed. He's alive!"
c) "One who lives for pleasure is dead even while alive."
d) "The body without the spirit is dead."

Level 11

Who first encouraged George Whitefield to visit the United States and preach there?

a) Benjamin Franklin
b) John and Charles Wesley
c) Jonathan Edwards
d) Oliver Cromwell

Gold

What was the title of Mahalia Jackson's first major successful song recording?

a) "God Gonna Separate the Wheat from the Tares"
b) "I'm Going to Move On Up a Little Higher"
c) "Precious Lord, Hold My Hand"
d) "Abraham, Martin, and John"

Pages 346–348 Pages 358–360 Pages 370–372 Pages 382–384

THIRTY INTERACTIVE QUIZZES THAT PUT YOU IN THE HOT SEAT

TRIVIA FOR LIFE

QUIZ 3

LEVEL 1

What is one of the principles that Martin Luther believed about Christianity?

a) A believer is justified by his or her works.
b) Christians have direct access to God.
c) Christians should be guided by law, gospel, and Church heritage.
d) Believers could receive revelation through dreams.

LEVEL 2

Clara Barton was the founder of what organization?

a) YMCA
b) Salvation Army
c) The Sanitary Commission
d) American Red Cross

Pages 337–338 Pages 349–350 Pages 361–362 Pages 373–374

LEVEL 3

Who is the artist of *Creation of Adam* in the Sistine Chapel?

a) Michelangelo
b) Albrecht Dürer
c) Leonardo da Vinci
d) Roger Tory Peterson

BRONZE

What does Mary Magdalene have to do with the number seven?

a) She kept watch at the tomb of Jesus for seven days.
b) She had seven demons driven from her.
c) Jesus told her to forgive seven times seventy.
d) She provided seven loaves to feed the multitude.

LEVEL 5

Where does Julia Ward Howe say that Jesus was born in her song "Battle Hymn of the Republic"?

a) in a papyrus basket
b) in the beauty of the lilies
c) in a manger
d) as a rose of Sharon

LEVEL 6

How were Esther and Mordecai related?

a) husband and wife
b) brother and sister
c) cousins
d) father and daughter

Pages 339–342 Pages 351–354 Pages 363–366 Pages 375–378

Level 7

What title could be used to describe Charles Spurgeon?

a) missionary exemplar
b) great orator
c) abolitionist and reformer
d) Father of English Protestantism

Silver

Why did Joseph of the Old Testament go to Egypt?

a) He was sold as a slave into Egypt.
b) His parents took him to Egypt to avoid those who sought to kill him.
c) He went into Egypt to tell Pharaoh to release his people.
d) He went into Egypt in his old age because of a famine.

Level 9

In addition to abolition of slavery, what other cause did Sojourner Truth champion?

a) retirement benefits for Civil War veterans
b) women's rights
c) nursing and hospital reform
d) child welfare

Pages 343–345 Pages 355–357 Pages 367–369 Pages 379–381

Level 10

What book did Dietrich Bonhoeffer finish while in a German prison?

a) *The Cost of Discipleship*
b) *A Testament from Prison*
c) *The Sacrifice from Cell 92*
d) *Principles of a Pacifist*

Level 11

To whom did Priscilla and her husband explain the way of God more adequately?

a) Demetrius
b) Barnabas
c) Lydia
d) Apollos

Gold

What was one of Amy Carmichael's primary activities?

a) rescuing girls who had been dedicated to pagan temples
b) protecting the intellectual property of songwriters
c) prohibiting the sale of alcohol
d) abolishing slavery

Pages 346–348 Pages 358–360 Pages 370–372 Pages 382–384

QUIZ 4

Level 1

The William and Gloria Gaither song "There's Something about That Name" refers to what specific name?

a) Jesus
b) Lion of Judah
c) the family of God
d) gentle Shepherd

Level 2

What did Aaron do for his brother Moses?

a) remained in Midian to care for Moses' flocks
b) was the orator for the words of Moses
c) laid his hands on Joshua as a replacement for Moses
d) disputed with the archangel Michael about the body of Moses

Pages 337–338 Pages 349–350 Pages 361–362 Pages 373–374

Level 3

For what crops did George Washington Carver develop new uses?

a) strawberries and blueberries
b) cotton and flax
c) corn and rice
d) peanuts and sweet potatoes

Bronze

In the refrain of "There Is Power in the Blood," how does Lewis Ellis Jones describe the power?

a) "cleansing"
b) "wonder working"
c) "purer"
d) "everlasting"

Level 5

Who did John the Baptist call a brood of vipers?

a) the apostles of Jesus
b) the Roman authorities
c) the Pharisees and Saddducees
d) the people of Nazareth

Pages 339–341 Pages 351–353 Pages 363–365 Pages 375–377

Level 6

In his song, what does Charles Wesley desire in order to sing "My great Redeemer's praise"?

a) "a golden voice"
b) "a mountaintop"
c) "majestic words"
d) "a thousand tongues"

Level 7

Why did Frederick Bailey take the name Frederick Douglass?

a) to conceal his shame at being the son of a white slaveholder
b) to bring honor to the man who helped him escape
c) to restore his true name from the one given him by his slave master
d) to make it more difficult to be traced as a runaway slave

Silver

How many of Eve's sons are named in the Bible?

a) none
b) two
c) three
d) seven

Level 9

What was Rebekah doing when the servant came to find a wife for Isaac?

a) bringing garments to be washed
b) driving cattle to pasture
c) carrying a jar for water
d) gathering firewood

Pages 342–345 Pages 354–357 Pages 366–369 Pages 378–381

Level 10

What period of time is *not* mentioned in the song "Amazing Grace" by John Newton?

a) days
b) month
c) hour
d) ten thousand years

Level 11

Which statement is true about R. G. LeTourneau?

a) He gave up a promising business career to become a missionary.
b) He began a publishing firm to provide missionary material in the French language.
c) He sold his companies rather than build weapons of war.
d) He was an industrialist who tithed 90 percent of his income.

Gold

What was Eric Liddell's nickname?

a) Galloping Ghost
b) Little Magician
c) Lost Dutchman
d) Flying Scotsman

Pages 346–348 Pages 358–360 Pages 370–372 Pages 382–384

THIRTY INTERACTIVE QUIZZES THAT PUT YOU IN THE HOT SEAT

TRIVIA FOR LIFE

QUIZ 5

LEVEL 1

How did the father of John the Baptist communicate the name of his son to his relatives?

a) He wrote on a tablet.
b) He whispered to his wife.
c) He pointed to a prophecy in scripture.
d) He wrote in the sand.

LEVEL 2

Billy Graham's preaching tours are known by what name?

a) campaigns
b) rallies
c) crusades
d) gospel meetings

Pages 337–338 Pages 349–350 Pages 361–362 Pages 373–374

Level 3

What employment did Dwight L. Moody leave to begin his religious activity?

a) train conductor
b) postal employee
c) shoe salesman
d) baseball player

Bronze

From what was Eve's first covering made?

a) garments of skin
b) woven flax and barley straw
c) fig leaves
d) knitted material of linen and wool

Level 5

Why did Eric Liddell miss the 1924 Olympic 100-meter race, his best event?

a) He wanted Harold Abrahams to win.
b) He was disqualified because he had been born in China.
c) He missed the taxi taking him to the event.
d) He chose not to run on Sunday.

Pages 339–341 Pages 351–353 Pages 363–365 Pages 375–377

Level 6

Which of David's wives is mentioned in Matthew?

a) Ahinoam
b) Abigail
c) Uriah's wife (Bathsheba)
d) Michal

Level 7

What follows the phrase "Rescue the perishing" in the refrain of the Fanny Crosby hymn of the same name?

a) "throw out the lifeline"
b) "pray for the harvest"
c) "care for the dying"
d) "look to the Savior"

Silver

After accepting the presidency of the College of New Jersey (later Princeton University), how did Jonathan Edwards die?

a) from a smallpox inoculation
b) at the hands of an angry mob
c) while trying to rescue his wife from their burning home
d) of a stroke while delivering an impassioned sermon

Pages 342–344 Pages 354–356 Pages 366–368 Pages 378–380

Level 9

Who was Silas?
- a) a teacher of Priscilla and Aquila
- b) the father of Timothy
- c) Paul's traveling companion
- d) John the Baptist's chief disciple

Level 10

How did Philip approach the chariot of the Ethiopian eunuch?
- a) while running
- b) while riding a camel
- c) being carried there in a whirlwind
- d) while waiting at an oasis

Level 11

What did Mary Slessor do for the British in Calabar, Nigeria?
- a) select routes for trading in palm oil
- b) arbitrate disputes between native tribes
- c) spy on German activities during World War I
- d) explore the Zambezi River

Gold

Whose scientific work did Jonathan Edwards read with great interest?
- a) Benjamin Franklin's
- c) Archimedes'
- b) Isaac Newton's
- d) Michael Faraday's

Pages 345–348 Pages 357–360 Pages 369–372 Pages 381–384

QUIZ 6

LEVEL 1

In Charlotte Elliott's song "Just as I Am," how many pleas did she have?

a) not one
b) one
c) seven times seventy
d) all

LEVEL 2

Henry Ward Beecher's sister Harriet was the author of what book?

a) *John Brown's Body*
b) *Poor Laws and Paupers*
c) *Uncle Tom's Cabin*
d) *Incidents in the Life of a Slave Girl*

Pages 337–338 Pages 349–350 Pages 361–362 Pages 373–374

Level 3

What kind of accident caused Joni Eareckson Tada to be paralyzed?

a) fall from her horse
b) diving accident while swimming
c) automobile accident late at night
d) sports injury while playing lacrosse

Bronze

Where was the mansion located in the Ira Stanphill song?

a) just over the hilltop
b) beside still waters
c) in a valley below
d) on level ground

Level 5

The statement "Your people will be my people and your God my God" was made by Ruth to whom?

a) David
b) Boaz
c) Naomi
d) village elders

Pages 339–341 Pages 351–353 Pages 363–365 Pages 375–377

Level 6

While Jesus visited Martha and her family at Bethany, what was true about the housework?

a) Martha left it undone to listen to Jesus.
b) Martha sent a servant girl to hire a room in which to serve Jesus.
c) Martha was distracted by it.
d) Neighbors helped Martha do the housework.

Level 7

How did Paul escape from those who waited to kill him as he left Damascus?

a) through a tunnel
b) being let down from the wall in a basket
c) an angel blinded the eyes of his enemies
d) in the confusion of an earthquake

Silver

Joseph Lister was a Christian and great surgeon who is credited with what medical discovery?

a) vaccination against smallpox
b) blood transfusion
c) anesthesia
d) antiseptic surgery

Pages 342–344 Pages 354–356 Pages 366–368 Pages 378–380

LEVEL 9

What action ensured that *My Utmost for His Highest* by Oswald Chambers was published?

a) Robert Louis Stevenson gave a favorable review.
b) Chambers wrote it while in quarantine.
c) Charles Spurgeon rescued the manuscript from a trash container.
d) Gertrude Hobbs, his wife, transcribed his lectures.

LEVEL 10

Which C. S. Lewis book is about his marriage late in life?

a) *Till We Have Faces*
b) *Allegory of Love*
c) *Surprised by Joy*
d) *Beyond Personality*

LEVEL 11

What was the religion of Watchman Nee's parents and grandparents?

a) Islam
b) Christianity
c) Confucianism
d) Buddhism

GOLD

What native custom did Mary Slessor battle in Africa?

a) exposure of the elderly
b) murder of twin babies
c) poaching of elephants for their ivory
d) blood rites to seal agreements

Pages 345–348 Pages 357–360 Pages 369–372 Pages 381–384

THIRTY INTERACTIVE QUIZZES THAT PUT YOU IN THE HOT SEAT

TRIVIA FOR LIFE

QUIZ 7

LEVEL 1

What was the hiding place referred to in Corrie ten Boom's book?

a) a secret room
b) a childhood nursery rhyme
c) a tree house
d) a shelter for battered women

LEVEL 2

After the Sabbath, what did Salome, Mary Magdalene, and Mary the mother of James take to the tomb of Jesus?

a) spices
b) burial linens
c) olive branches and flowers
d) marker of stones for His tomb

Pages 337–338 Pages 349–350 Pages 361–362 Pages 373–374

Level 3

What United States holiday has its roots in a celebration Priscilla Mullins and her future husband, John Alden, attended when it was first held?

a) Independence Day
b) Thanksgiving
c) Christmas
d) Columbus Day

Bronze

In what river did John the Baptist preach and baptize?

a) Tigris
b) Pishon
c) Jordan
d) Hebron

Level 5

What did Jesus do for the widow who lived in the town of Nain?

a) went to eat in her house
b) granted her justice against her adversary
c) healed her of a disease she had suffered for twelve years
d) raised her only son from the dead

Pages 339–341 Pages 351–353 Pages 363–365 Pages 375–377

Level 6

Why did Dante Alighieri write *The Divine Comedy* in Italian rather than Latin?

a) He was forbidden to publish in Latin.
b) He preferred to write in the language of the common people.
c) Anything ancient repelled him.
d) It was the only language he knew.

Level 7

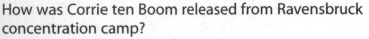

How was Corrie ten Boom released from Ravensbruck concentration camp?

a) by a clerical error
b) American soldiers liberated her
c) through her death
d) by a guard who had become a Christian

Silver

What book did Watchman Nee begin writing at the age of twenty-three?

a) *The Normal Christian Life*
b) *The Spiritual Man*
c) *Love Not the World*
d) *A Living Sacrifice*

Pages 342–344 Pages 354–356 Pages 366–368 Pages 378–380

LEVEL 9

How long did Moses' mother hide him after he was born?

a) three months
b) seven weeks
c) twelve years
d) forty days

LEVEL 10

What name could be applied to Watchman Nee?

a) Great Commoner
b) Blind Evangelist
c) Sportsman Christian
d) Man of Suffering

LEVEL 11

Before devoting himself fully to religious matters, what did Blaise Pascal study with Pierre de Fermat?

a) the orbits of planets
b) the classification of plants
c) the speed of falling bodies
d) problems involving probability and statistics

GOLD

Rebekah received what kind of gifts from the servant sent to find a wife for Isaac?

a) nose ring and bracelets
b) honey, pistachio nuts, and almonds
c) sweet cakes
d) goats and sheep

Pages 345–348 Pages 357–360 Pages 369–372 Pages 381–384

QUIZ 8

LEVEL 1

Why did God not let David build the temple (house of God)?

a) Israel under David was too poor.
b) David had become too old and weak.
c) David had shed much blood.
d) David could not unite warring tribes.

LEVEL 2

What is the title of the William J. and Gloria Gaither song that explains why "I can face tomorrow"?

a) "Jesus, We Just Want to Thank You"
b) "Because He Lives"
c) "A Hill Called Mount Calvary"
d) "His Name Is Life"

Pages 337–338 Pages 349–350 Pages 361–362 Pages 373–374

LEVEL 3

Which New Testament male has his lineage traced through Ruth?

a) the Ethiopian
b) Cornelius
c) Saul (Paul)
d) Joseph, the husband of Mary

BRONZE

In Frances Ridlex Havergal's song, what words come after "I gave My life for thee"?

a) "with thorns upon My head"
b) "My precious blood I shed"
c) "come ye blessed"
d) "I bring rich gifts to thee"

LEVEL 5

Which Nobel Prize did Teresa of Calcutta receive in 1979?

a) peace
b) literature
c) medicine
d) economics

Pages 339–341 Pages 351–353 Pages 363–365 Pages 375–377

Level 6

What was the first question that Philip asked the Ethiopian eunuch riding in the chariot?

a) "Do you understand what you are reading?"
b) "Do you speak Greek?"
c) "What do you have to do with the Lord, the God of Israel?"
d) "Do you think you will escape God's judgment?"

Level 7

What city does Christian leave in John Bunyan's *The Pilgrim's Progress*?

a) City of the Dead
b) Babylon
c) City of Destruction
d) City of Ignorance

Silver

What special job did the district ruler in China give to Gladys Aylward?

a) foot inspector
b) tea taster
c) mule skinner
d) bookkeeper

Level 9

Who was the Native American who became a Christian and gave assistance to the Plymouth Colony settlers?

a) Squanto
b) Aunt Queen
c) Thomas Dusta
d) Pocahontas

Pages 342–345 Pages 354–357 Pages 366–369 Pages 378–381

LEVEL 10

What phrase completes this statement by Hudson Taylor: "Under no circumstance would the missionary effort. . ."?

a) "incur debt."
b) "be done by unmarried female missionaries."
c) "be conducted by married male missionaries."
d) "accept funds from abroad."

LEVEL 11

What did Martha, the sister of Lazarus, do when she heard that Jesus was coming to their house?

a) She dressed in a veil to receive Him.
b) She cleaned the house.
c) She went outside to meet Him.
d) She started to cry.

GOLD

What description has been applied to John Wycliffe?

a) Lollard of Coventry
b) Lion of Oxford
c) morning star of the Reformation
d) Luther's bulldog

Pages 346–348 Pages 358–360 Pages 370–372 Pages 382–384

THIRTY INTERACTIVE QUIZZES THAT PUT YOU IN THE HOT SEAT

TRIVIA FOR LIFE

QUIZ 9

Level 1

What phrase describes how "Jesus is calling" in Will L. Thompson's song?

a) "softly and tenderly"
b) "with love divine"
c) "with steadfast spirit"
d) "with enduring mercy"

Level 2

In what city did John Calvin develop his religious ideas?

a) Venice, Italy
b) Tübingen, Germany
c) Paris, France
d) Geneva, Switzerland

Pages 337–338 Pages 349–350 Pages 361–362 Pages 373–374

Level 3

What was the question Nicodemus asked of Jesus?

a) "Am I my brother's keeper?"
b) "Sir, what must I do to be saved?"
c) "How can a man be born when he is old?"
d) "Tell me, are you a Roman citizen?"

Bronze

In what area was Charles G. Finney's greatest success?

a) providing assistance to the poor and suffering
b) bringing the gospel to Native Americans
c) as a revival evangelist
d) organizing and promoting Sunday schools

Level 5

Which Pharisee came to Jesus late at night?

a) Joseph of Arimathea
b) Zacchaeus
c) Nicodemus
d) James Zebedee

Level 6

Who was the Christian scientist who stated the relationship between the pressure and volume of a gas?

a) Marie Curie
b) Humphry Davy
c) William Perkin
d) Robert Boyle

Pages 339–342 Pages 351–354 Pages 363–366 Pages 375–378

Level 7

What kind of house is mentioned in the song "Let the Lower Lights Be Burning" by Philip P. Bliss?

a) lighthouse
b) farmhouse
c) house of God
d) house built on sand

Silver

How is Charles Sheldon's book *In His Steps* best described?

a) a collection of sermons
b) inspirational fiction
c) a biography of Carry Nation
d) one week in the life of a Christian newspaper editor

Level 9

In her hymn "I Am Thine, O Lord," what appeal did Fanny J. Crosby make?

a) "make me worthy"
b) "draw me nearer"
c) "give me a mansion"
d) "keep me content"

Pages 343–345 Pages 355–357 Pages 367–369 Pages 379–381

Level 10

What was the original title of the song "Amazing Grace" by John Newton?

a) "Blinded in Youth by Satan's Arts"
b) "Faith's Review and Expectation"
c) "Be Still, My Heart! These Anxious Cares"
d) "Alas! By Nature How Depraved"

Level 11

Although she was British, Florence Nightingale was born in which country?

a) Portugal
b) Turkey
c) Egypt
d) Italy

Gold

Astronaut James B. Irwin began what Christian evangelistic organization?

a) Open Skies
b) Chariots of Fire
c) High Flight Foundation
d) Scripture Memory Fellowship

Pages 346–348 Pages 358–360 Pages 370–372 Pages 382–384

QUIZ 10

LEVEL 1

In Eugene M. Bartlett's song, what was found "in Jesus"?

a) "the gates to life"
b) "victory"
c) "a lifeline"
d) "sleep"

LEVEL 2

The book *In His Steps* by Charles Sheldon is the basis for what question?

a) Will You bless me, too, my father?
b) Am I my brother's keeper?
c) What would Jesus do?
d) Which is the greatest commandment in the Law?

Pages 337–338 Pages 349–350 Pages 361–362 Pages 373–374

Level 3

What did the woman do who had been bleeding for twelve years?

a) prepared Jesus a meal of bread, curds, and milk
b) touched the edge of Jesus' cloak
c) poured perfume on the head of Jesus
d) washed the feet of Jesus with her hair

Bronze

In his song, where does Russell Kelso Carter shout and sing that he is standing?

a) in Canaan's land
b) on the promises of God
c) on streets of gold
d) on Jordan's banks

Level 5

Florence Nightingale's nursing activity is associated primarily with what war?

a) Crimean War
b) American Civil War
c) Napoleonic Wars
d) Boer War

Pages 339–341 Pages 351–353 Pages 363–365 Pages 375–377

Level 6

What was the purpose of the underground to which Corrie ten Boom and her family belonged?

a) to free slaves
b) to provide a safe haven for Jews
c) to transport German sympathizers
d) to give gypsies a way to earn a living

Level 7

The song "Jesus, Hold My Hand" by Albert E. Brumley begins with what phrase?

a) "As I travel through this pilgrim land"
b) "Now I am climbing higher each day"
c) "To a land where joy never ends"
d) "I'm bound for that city"

Silver

Where is Leonardo da Vinci's painting *The Last Supper* located?

a) Royal Library, Windsor Castle, England
b) Musée du Louvre, Paris
c) Santa Maria delle Grazie in Milan, Italy
d) the Sistine Chapel, Vatican, Italy

Pages 342–344 Pages 354–356 Pages 366–368 Pages 378–380

Level 9

What word is missing from the phrase "___ of love" in Fanny J. Crosby's song "Blessed Assurance"?

a) "song"
b) "shadow"
c) "light"
d) "purchase"

Level 10

Clara Barton's training and experience were in what field?

a) bookkeeping
b) school teaching
c) nursing
d) singing

Level 11

What commendation did Enoch receive before he was taken from this life?

a) as one who pleased God
b) as a great warrior
c) as being a just king
d) as caring for his poor neighbors

Gold

What African-American wrote "Peace in the Valley"?

a) Charles Richard Drew
b) Thomas A. Dorsey
c) Harriet Tubman
d) William C. Handy

Pages 345–348 Pages 357–360 Pages 369–372 Pages 381–384

THIRTY INTERACTIVE QUIZZES THAT PUT YOU IN THE HOT SEAT

TRIVIA FOR LIFE

QUIZ 11

LEVEL 1

What is the missing word from martyr Betty Scott Stam's motto: For to me, to live is Christ, and to die is _____?

a) victory
b) glory
c) power
d) gain

LEVEL 2

In Ira F. Stanphill's song "I Know Who Holds Tomorrow," what word completes the line "And I know who holds my…"?

a) "heart."
b) "hand."
c) "future."
d) "happiness."

Pages 337–338 Pages 349–350 Pages 361–362 Pages 373–374

Level 3

Who was the Christian believer who stated the law of universal gravitation?

a) Isaac Newton
b) Galileo
c) Edmund Halley
d) John Hooke

Bronze

From what is William W. Walford called in his song "Sweet Hour of Prayer"?

a) "from a life unaware"
b) "from a world of care"
c) "from an easy chair"
d) "from the devil's snare"

Level 5

What was John Bunyan's position when he began writing *The Pilgrim's Progress*?

a) vice chancellor at Oxford University
b) prisoner in the Bedford, England, jail
c) secretary of the admiralty in London
d) soldier in Cromwell's army

Level 6

From what region was the leper who came back to thank Jesus for his healing?

a) Rome
b) Samaria
c) Galilee
d) Egypt

Pages 339–342 Pages 351–354 Pages 363–366 Pages 375–378

LEVEL 7

What name could be applied to Brother Andrew (Andy van der Bijl)?

a) Opponent of the Nazi Regime
b) Great Revivalist
c) Missionary to Liberia
d) God's Undercover Agent

SILVER

For what purpose did Agabus take Paul's belt?

a) to return it to Carpus at Troas, who had lent it to Paul
b) to prophesy how Paul would be bound in Jerusalem
c) to prevent Paul from leaving Caesarea
d) to take it to Philip's four daughters so they could prophesy by touching it

LEVEL 9

What did Philip say to overcome his brother Nathaniel's disbelief that Jesus was the Messiah?

a) "Never spake one like this."
b) "Come and see."
c) "He is like one crying in the wilderness."
d) "He took away the sins of the world."

Pages 343–345 Pages 355–357 Pages 367–369 Pages 379–381

Level 10

What did Ezra devote himself to?
- a) study and teaching the commands of God
- b) assembling a mighty army
- c) building a watchtower to protect the city
- d) tracing his lineage back to Adam

Level 11

What was the name of Dante's fictionalized woman in *The Divine Comedy*?
- a) Deborah
- b) Gemma di Manetto Donati
- c) Veronica
- d) Beatrice

Gold

Who was the Christian believer who showed that light is made of electromagnetic waves?
- a) James Clerk Maxwell
- b) Christian Huygens
- c) Albert Michelson
- d) John Dalton

Pages 346–348 Pages 358–360 Pages 370–372 Pages 382–384

Quiz 12

Level 1

For what activity is evangelist Charles Wesley known?

a) organizing congregations
b) writing hymns
c) translating the works of Martin Luther
d) delivering sermons

Level 2

The hymn "When the Roll Is Called Up Yonder" by James Milton Black mentions what musical instrument in the first line?

a) cymbals
b) lyre
c) trumpet
d) harp

Pages 337–338 Pages 349–350 Pages 361–362 Pages 373–374

Level 3

In the James Rowe song "Love Lifted Me," what was he far from?

a) "the peaceful shore"
b) "home of the soul"
c) "cliff of the rock"
d) "lights of home"

Bronze

What did God state about Eve's offspring?

a) That He would crush the serpent's head.
b) That He would be a little lower than the angels.
c) That He would begin a people too numerous to count.
d) That He would be called a "son of the living God."

Level 5

In what country did William Carey serve for forty-one years?

a) India
b) China
c) Africa
d) Canada

Level 6

Who was the Christian believer and great scientist who discovered a vaccination for rabies?

a) Joseph Lister
b) Edward Jenner
c) Roger Bacon
d) Louis Pasteur

Pages 339–342 Pages 351–354 Pages 363–366 Pages 375–378

LEVEL 7

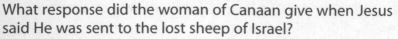

What response did the woman of Canaan give when Jesus said He was sent to the lost sheep of Israel?

a) "The shepherd leaves the ninety-nine and goes after the lost sheep."
b) "I give half of my possessions to the poor."
c) "It is not the healthy who need a doctor, but the sick."
d) "Even the dogs eat the crumbs that fall from their masters' table."

SILVER

Because they were both from Scotland and worked in textile mills as children, who did Mary Slessor identify with as her exemplar missionary?

a) Hudson Taylor
b) Gladys Aylward
c) David Livingstone
d) George Müller

LEVEL 9

What step did Hudson Taylor take to be a more effective missionary?

a) He dressed as a native teacher.
b) He built a walled city as a Christian stronghold.
c) He translated Chinese literature into English.
d) He used puppet plays to tell the story of Jesus.

Pages 343–345 Pages 355–357 Pages 367–369 Pages 379–381

Level 10

What condition did English poet William Cowper, author of "There Is a Fountain," struggle with?

a) alcoholism
b) blindness
c) depression
d) deafness

Level 11

William Carey had exceptional ability in what position?

a) school superintendent
b) translator
c) governor
d) hospital administrator

Gold

How did Dietrich Bonhoeffer die?

a) of pneumonia while an honored guest in Britain
b) by hanging at a concentration camp
c) at home during the bombing of Berlin
d) aboard a ship sunk by a U-boat

Pages 346–348 Pages 358–360 Pages 370–372 Pages 382–384

THIRTY INTERACTIVE QUIZZES THAT PUT YOU IN THE HOT SEAT

TRIVIA FOR LIFE

QUIZ 13

LEVEL 1

Who is the title character in *The Screwtape Letters* by C. S. Lewis?

a) an experienced devil
b) the nephew of the letter writer
c) an English linguist named Ransom
d) C. S. Lewis himself

LEVEL 2

What did John the Baptist eat in the wilderness?

a) fish
b) bread and water
c) locusts and wild honey
d) figs and pomegranates

Pages 337–338 Pages 349–350 Pages 361–362 Pages 373–375

LEVEL 3

What organization did William and Catherine Booth found?

a) Teen Challenge
b) Red Cross
c) YMCA
d) Salvation Army

BRONZE

In the song "Farther Along" by W. B. Stevens, what follows "Cheer up my brother"?

a) "every step is getting brighter"
b) "look to realms above"
c) "live in the sunshine"
d) "soon we'll reach the shining river"

LEVEL 5

Gladys Aylward served in what occupation before going to China?

a) a nurse
b) a schoolteacher
c) a maid
d) an actress

Pages 339–341 Pages 351–353 Pages 363–365 Pages 375–377

LEVEL 6

Why did Rhoda delay opening the door when Peter escaped from prison?

a) She feared the Romans.
b) She thought he was a ghost.
c) She thought she would be laughed at.
d) She was overjoyed.

LEVEL 7

What was the first public message sent by Samuel F. B. Morse's telegraph?

a) "What hath God wrought!"
b) the words of "Silent Night"
c) "Lord, who has believed our message?"
d) "Your lightning lit up the world."

SILVER

How old was Anna when she saw Jesus in the temple?

a) 12 years old
b) 33 years old
c) 40 years old
d) 84 years old

Pages 342–344 Pages 354–356 Pages 366–368 Pages 378–380

Level 9

Dietrich Bonhoeffer was an outspoken leader of which church that opposed Hitler and Nazism?

a) Non-Aryan Christian Church
b) German Evangelical Church
c) National Socialist Church
d) Confessing Church

Level 10

Why was Hezekiah like no king of Judah either before or after him?

a) Only God was held in greater respect by the people.
b) He followed the Lord and kept the commands given to Moses.
c) He did evil in the eyes of the Lord continually.
d) Peace reigned throughout Canaan.

Level 11

Which of these heroes of faith did not experience death?

a) Samson
b) Enoch
c) Gideon
d) Jacob

Gold

Edith Schaeffer's first book about her and her husband's work in Switzerland carried what title?

a) *Children for Christ*
b) *Defending the Faith*
c) *The Tapestry*
d) *L'Abri* (the shelter)

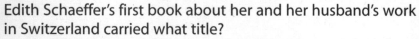

Pages 345–348 Pages 357–360 Pages 369–372 Pages 381–384

Quiz 14

Level 1

Why did Joseph continue with his plans to take Mary as his wife?

a) he had a visit from an angel
b) to escape the wrath of the village elders
c) to inherit her extensive dowry
d) to fulfill a promise he had given her father

Level 2

Who named all the animals on earth?

a) Shem's sons at Babel
b) Adam
c) God
d) Noah

Pages 337–338 Pages 349–350 Pages 361–362 Pages 373–374

Level 3

What is the title of Jonathan Edwards's sermon that says "there is nothing between you and Hell but the air"?

a) "True Virtue"
b) "A Strict Enquiry into Notions of Freedom of Will"
c) "Sinners in the Hands of an Angry God"
d) "God Glorified in Man's Dependence"

Bronze

What was Andrew's relation to Simon Peter?

a) hired servant
b) father
c) son
d) brother

Level 5

In what war did Clara Barton earn the title "angel of the battlefield"?

a) Spanish-American War
b) American Civil War
c) World War I
d) Franco-Prussian War

Level 6

After learning that Jesus was the Messiah, what did Andrew do?

a) asked to be healed
b) told his brother
c) asked to sit on Jesus' right hand
d) fished all night

Pages 339–342 Pages 351–354 Pages 363–366 Pages 375–378

Level 7

Francis Schaeffer is noted for defending the historical accuracy of what portion of Scripture?

a) The biblical account of Moses
b) Genesis 1–11
c) The biblical account of Jesus
d) The biblical account of Abraham

Silver

Who watched baby Moses while he was being hidden from Pharaoh?

a) his father
b) his brother Aaron
c) his sister Miriam
d) his grandmother

Level 9

How is Samuel Morris (Prince Kaboo) described on his memorial at Taylor University?

a) Liberator of Liberia
b) King of Missionaries
c) Man Without a Country
d) Apostle of Simple Faith

Pages 343–345 Pages 355–357 Pages 367–369 Pages 379–381

Level 10

Of what religious movement was George Whitefield one of the leaders?

a) Protestant Reformation
b) Great Awakening
c) Moderate Sensibility
d) Backwoods Revivalism

Level 11

What title could be used to describe Luis Palau's early ministry?

a) The Singing Cowboy
b) Argentina's hymn writer
c) Evangelist of Latin America
d) Survivor of the Inquisition

Gold

What was the primary reason Frederick Douglass wrote *Narrative of the Life of Frederick Douglass*?

a) to establish himself as a writer
b) to help locate his family
c) to provide specific details of his life to prove that he had been a slave
d) to raise money for abolitionist causes

Pages 346–348 Pages 358–360 Pages 370–372 Pages 382–384

THIRTY INTERACTIVE QUIZZES THAT PUT YOU IN THE HOT SEAT

TRIVIA FOR LIFE

QUIZ 15

Level 1

Brother Andrew (Andy van der Bijl) first smuggled Bibles into what part of the world?

a) behind the Iron Curtain
b) Red China
c) the Muslim world
d) Africa

Level 2

What words of Jesus does Leonardo da Vinci illustrate with *The Last Supper*?

a) "The Christ will suffer and rise from the dead on the third day."
b) "Unless I wash you, you have no part with me."
c) "Before the rooster crows, you will disown me three times."
d) "One of you will betray me—one who is eating with me."

Pages 337–338 Pages 349–350 Pages 361–362 Pages 373–374

LEVEL 3

In Charles Wesley's song "Hark, the Herald Angels Sing," what do the angels sing?

a) "a new song in heaven"
b) "everyone is awaiting the coming day"
c) "take time to praise the Lord"
d) "glory to the newborn King"

BRONZE

What physical condition affected Fanny J. Crosby?

a) severe depression
b) quadriplegia
c) muscular dystrophy
d) blindness

LEVEL 5

Who was the three-time presidential candidate who wrote *The Bible and Its Enemies*?

a) Jimmy Carter
b) James Garfield
c) James Buchanan
d) William Jennings Bryan

LEVEL 6

What was the source of George Müller's salary?

a) unsolicited freewill offerings
b) his father's dynamite business
c) his many best-selling books
d) his wife's inheritance

Pages 339–342 Pages 351–354 Pages 363–366 Pages 375–378

Level 7

Who was Zipporah's husband, whom she described as "an Egyptian" when they first met?

a) Moses
b) Joshua
c) Noah
d) Joseph

Silver

In the William Cowper song that has the phrase "His wonders to perform," how does he say that God moves?

a) "with an easy yoke"
b) "softly and tenderly"
c) "in a mysterious way"
d) "as footprints in the sand"

Level 9

What organization did George Müller found?

a) The Navigators
b) Scriptural Knowledge Institution
c) National Home Education Association
d) Society of Friends

Pages 343–345 Pages 355–357 Pages 367–369 Pages 379–381

Level 10

The well where Jesus talked with a woman of Samaria was named after what Old Testament person?

a) Noah
b) Jonah
c) Gideon
d) Jacob

Level 11

George Washington Carver said, "_____ is an unlimited broadcasting system through which God speaks to us every hour, if we will only tune in."

a) "Nature"
b) "Prayer"
c) "The Bible"
d) "The starry sky"

Gold

By what name were Charles Wesley and his friends known at Oxford University?

a) Wesley's Party
b) Holy Club
c) Faithful Brethren
d) Singing Saints

Pages 346–348 Pages 358–360 Pages 370–372 Pages 382–384

QUIZ 16

LEVEL 1

What term did Teresa of Calcutta use for the poor, sick, and suffering?

a) street people
b) slum brothers and sisters
c) Christ in disguise
d) congregation of the destitute

LEVEL 2

What is the subtitle of the book *Ben-Hur* by Lew Wallace?

a) *A Tale of the Christ*
b) *The First Christmas*
c) *The Chariot Race*
d) *A Prince of Israel*

Pages 337–338 Pages 349–350 Pages 361–362 Pages 373–374

Level 3

What did God tell Abraham about Sarah?

a) Her son would be a joy and delight.
b) The Spirit of God would come upon her.
c) She would be the mother of nations.
d) She had found favor with God.

Bronze

What was Abel's occupation?

a) laborer in the fields
b) mighty warrior
c) tender of vineyards
d) keeper of flocks

Level 5

While in a trance, what did Peter hear God tell him to do?

a) stay awake until the rooster crowed
b) fast for forty days
c) warm himself by the enemy's fire
d) kill and eat unclean animals

Level 6

How did William Tyndale die?

a) he was strangled and burned at the stake
b) of an illness while visiting the Holy Land
c) ill treatment while in prison
d) lost at sea while transporting New Testaments to England

Pages 339–342 Pages 351–354 Pages 363–366 Pages 375–378

LEVEL 7

In Robert Lowry's song "Beautiful River" ("Shall We Gather at the River"), whose feet trod along the river?

a) bright angel
b) Son of God
c) wayfaring pilgrims
d) those marching to Zion

SILVER

What did Edward "Buzz" Aldrin do when he and Neil Armstrong landed on the moon on Sunday, July 20, 1969?

a) read the "In the beginning" passage from Genesis
b) observed the Lord's Supper
c) recited the Lord's Prayer
d) sang a hymn

LEVEL 9

Why did Hannah choose the name Samuel for her son?

a) It means "hairy"—his appearance.
b) It means "perfection of the father"—he favored his father.
c) It means "brother of Ramuel"—his twin sister.
d) It means "asked of the LORD"—she prayed for a son.

Pages 343–345 Pages 355–357 Pages 367–369 Pages 379–381

Level 10

According to the writer of Hebrews, Abraham looked for what kind of city?

a) "a city on a hill"
b) "the city of the living God"
c) "a holy city with the tree of life"
d) "a city whose architect and builder is God"

Level 11

A. W. Tozer is the author of what book?

a) *Institutes of the Christian Religion*
b) *How to Be Born Again*
c) *The Pursuit of God*
d) *A Fully Surrendered Man*

Gold

What happened when Sojourner Truth brought suit in court for the return of her son, who had been sold into slavery in Alabama?

a) She lost and had to pay court costs.
b) She won the case.
c) Her case was dismissed without merit.
d) It went for years without resolution.

Pages 346–348 Pages 358–360 Pages 370–372 Pages 382–384

THIRTY INTERACTIVE QUIZZES THAT PUT YOU IN THE HOT SEAT

TRIVIA FOR LIFE

QUIZ 17

LEVEL 1

What scripture prompted Martin Luther to say, "At this I felt myself to have been born again"?

a) "This water symbolizes baptism that now saves you also."
b) "And those He predestined, He also called."
c) "If God is for us, who can be against us?"
d) "The righteous will live by faith."

LEVEL 2

What is Florence Nightingale often portrayed carrying?

a) pitcher of water
b) medical kit
c) lamp
d) Bible

Pages 337–338 Pages 349–350 Pages 361–362 Pages 373–374

LEVEL 3

The lines "Let every heart prepare Him room, and heaven and nature sing" is from what song by Isaac Watts?

a) "I'm Not Ashamed to Own My Lord"
b) "How Shall the Young Secure Their Hearts"
c) "There Is a Land of Pure Delight"
d) "Joy to the World"

BRONZE

In the Martin Luther hymn "A Mighty Fortress Is Our God," how does he identify the devil?

a) "our ancient foe"
b) "Lucifer"
c) "sly fox"
d) "Legion"

LEVEL 5

What best-selling book did Dale Evans write about Robin, her daughter with Down's Syndrome?

a) *Pals of the Golden West*
b) *Angel Unaware*
c) *Just Sing a Song*
d) *The Day That We Met Jesus*

LEVEL 6

To what does Albert E. Brumley liken himself in his song "He Set Me Free"?

a) bird in prison
b) a worm
c) a lost sheep
d) a lily of the valley

Pages 339–342 Pages 351–354 Pages 363–366 Pages 375–378

Level 7

What six-thousand-seat auditorium was built for Charles Haddon Spurgeon?

- a) Royal Albert Hall
- b) Metropolitan Tabernacle
- c) the Globe Theater
- d) the Crystal Palace

Silver

What do Susanna, Joanna, and Mary Magdalene have in common?

- a) They all belonged to the household of Herod.
- b) They were lepers.
- c) They helped support Jesus and the disciples.
- d) They encouraged their husbands in the faith.

Level 9

What did Gideon call the altar he built?

- a) "Here Is Faith"
- b) "The LORD Is Peace"
- c) "The Place I Saw an Angel"
- d) "The Wisdom of God"

Pages 343–345 Pages 355–357 Pages 367–369 Pages 379–381

Level 10

Who said, "He told me everything I ever did"?

a) nobleman whose son was sick at Capernaum
b) demon-possessed man from the tombs
c) Samaritan woman who met Jesus at the well
d) centurion whose servant was sick

Level 11

Why did Frederick Douglass go to England in 1859?

a) to escape the danger of seizure under the Fugitive Slave Laws
b) to gain support for the American Civil War
c) to avoid possible arrest because of John Brown's raid at Harpers Ferry
d) to raise money for Abraham Lincoln's campaign for president

Gold

Why did Andy van der Bijl minister under the name Brother Andrew?

a) to be harder to trace as he moved about an unfriendly country
b) to appear to be a local resident
c) because he admired Andrew in the Bible
d) to put his past behind him and start fresh

Pages 346–348 Pages 358–360 Pages 370–372 Pages 382–384

QUIZ 18

LEVEL 1

What movie chronicles the story of Eric Liddell's Olympic triumphs?

a) *Wings*
b) *A Step Farther*
c) *Chariots of Fire*
d) *Triumph of Will*

LEVEL 2

What was the name of the mother of John the Baptist?

a) Anna
b) Joanna
c) Elizabeth
d) Tabitha

Pages 337–338 Pages 349–350 Pages 361–362 Pages 373–374

Level 3

Who said "I will fear no evil"?

a) Noah as the rains descended
b) David in one of his psalms
c) John the Baptist when thrown into prison
d) Jonah before preaching to Nineveh

Bronze

In the Roy Rogers and Dale Evans song, what follows the opening words of "Happy trails to you..."

a) "for a life that is true."
b) "until we meet again."
c) "it's the way you ride the trail that counts."
d) "who cares about the clouds."

Level 5

Whom did the Lord describe to Satan as "There is no one on earth like him; he is blameless and upright"?

a) David
b) Moses
c) Job
d) Noah

Level 6

What person, known as the Father of Modern Missions, was trained as a shoemaker?

a) C. S. Lewis
b) Billy Graham
c) David Livingstone
d) William Carey

Pages 339–342 Pages 351–354 Pages 363–366 Pages 375–378

LEVEL 7

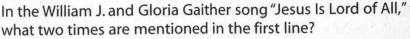

In the William J. and Gloria Gaither song "Jesus Is Lord of All," what two times are mentioned in the first line?

a) "the years and the ages"
b) "all my tomorrows, all my past"
c) "ages roll through eternity's scroll"
d) "a time to be born and a time to die"

SILVER

In addition to being an explorer and missionary, what was another of David Livingstone's occupations?

a) veterinarian
b) newspaper reporter
c) physician
d) songwriter

LEVEL 9

After being dismissed from his congregation in Northampton, Massachusetts, Jonathan Edwards served in what capacity?

a) as a newspaper editor in Philadelphia
b) as a naturalist growing new varieties of potatoes
c) as a missionary to Native Americans
d) as a translator of Luther's works from the German language

Pages 343–345 Pages 355–357 Pages 367–369 Pages 379–381

Level 10

Who wrote the book *Institutes of the Christian Religion,* which helped establish Protestantism?

a) Martin Luther
b) John Calvin
c) Ulrich Zwingli
d) John Knox

Level 11

What did Abraham do when God said his wife, Sarah, would have a son?

a) moved from Ur of the Chaldeans to Canaan
b) sacrificed a ram
c) built an altar to the Lord
d) fell facedown and laughed

Gold

Why did Paul refer to Phoebe as "our sister"?

a) She managed a home for orphans.
b) She was a servant of the church.
c) She was charitable to everyone.
d) She was Paul's half sister.

Pages 346–348 Pages 358–360 Pages 370–372 Pages 382–384

THIRTY INTERACTIVE QUIZZES THAT PUT YOU IN THE HOT SEAT

TRIVIA FOR LIFE

QUIZ 19

LEVEL 1

Where did Moses receive the Ten Commandments from God?

a) Mount Carmel
b) Mount Horeb
c) mountains of Ararat
d) Mount Sinai

LEVEL 2

What words are missing from this song by Thomas A. Dorsey: "Precious Lord, _________, lead me on"?

a) "thru the night"
b) "thru the storm"
c) "take my hand"
d) "to the light"

Pages 337–338 Pages 349–350 Pages 361–362 Pages 373–374

Level 3

In his song "Soldiers of Christ, Arise," what does Charles Wesley tell soldiers of Christ to do?

a) "march to Zion"
b) "sing Hail to the Risen Lord"
c) "to Christ be loyal"
d) "put your armor on"

Bronze

In Gloria Gaither's song "Something Beautiful," what did "He" understand?

a) "how to help us find our way"
b) "all my confusion"
c) "kings and kingdoms"
d) "battlefields of my own making"

Level 5

Johannes Kepler was a Christian who made what scientific discovery?

a) the three laws of planetary motion
b) matter is made of atoms
c) the principle of the pendulum
d) the speed of light in a vacuum

Pages 339–341 Pages 351–353 Pages 363–365 Pages 375–377

Level 6

What doctrine did John Wesley and his brother emphasize?
- a) contending for the faith
- b) predestination
- c) faith and the pursuit of holiness
- d) universal salvation

Level 7

What book, the first he wrote, is the starting point for understanding Francis Schaeffer's theology?
- a) *A Christian View of Ecology*
- b) *The God Who Is There*
- c) *False Antithesis*
- d) *A Christian Manifesto*

Silver

What did Samuel of the Old Testament answer when he realized the Lord was calling him?
- a) "Here I am; you called me."
- b) "What shall I do, Lord?"
- c) "O Lord, please send someone else."
- d) "Speak, for your servant is listening."

Pages 342–344 Pages 354–356 Pages 366–368 Pages 378–380

LEVEL 9

In addition to being a prophetess, what else is true about Deborah of the Old Testament?

a) She was the wife of Solomon.
b) She led Israel.
c) She was a priestess.
d) She earned a living by gleaning grain.

LEVEL 10

The line "and the white robed angels sing the story" is from what Charles Austin Miles song?

a) "A New Name in Glory"
b) "Look for Me!"
c) "I'm Going There"
d) "Dwelling in Beulah Land"

LEVEL 11

What was the purpose of Susanna Wesley's strong discipline and instruction for her children?

a) for a vocation worthy of a Wesley
b) for the saving of their souls
c) for acquiring a measure of riches
d) for their success as ministers

GOLD

What did Agabus prophesy when Paul was in Antioch?

a) a marriage in Cana
b) a great fire in Rome
c) Jesus' death
d) a severe famine

Pages 345–348 Pages 357–360 Pages 369–372 Pages 381–384

QUIZ 20

LEVEL 1

What is Billy Graham's primary focus in modern Christianity?

a) evangelism
b) foreign missions
c) song writing
d) philanthropy

LEVEL 2

What name was later given to the type of worship John Wesley and his brother began while at the University of Oxford?

a) Puritanism
b) Wesleyism
c) Moravianism
d) Methodism

Pages 337–338 Pages 349–350 Pages 361–362 Pages 373–374

LEVEL 3

What career did Billy Sunday have before becoming a minister?

a) professional baseball player
b) schoolteacher
c) telegraph operator
d) lumberjack

BRONZE

How is the book *The Pilgrim's Progress* by John Bunyan best described?

a) memoirs of a missionary
b) historical novel
c) devotional book
d) allegory

LEVEL 5

Sir Christopher Wren is noted for what accomplishment?

a) discovery of the planet Neptune
b) astronomer of the southern skies
c) author of *The Faerie Queene*
d) architect of Saint Paul's cathedral, London

Pages 339–341 Pages 351–353 Pages 363–365 Pages 375–377

LEVEL 6

Michael Faraday was a Christian who invented what important device?

a) telephone
b) solid fuel rocket
c) electric motor
d) precision chronometer

LEVEL 7

Who wrote *Paradise Regained,* the sequel to John Milton's *Paradise Lost*?

a) Francis Bacon
b) John Milton
c) Samuel Pepys
d) John Bunyan

SILVER

What is the name of the ministry that Brother Andrew (Andy van der Bijl) founded?

a) Bibles Without Borders
b) Open Doors
c) Undercover Missionaries
d) The Red Letter Edition

LEVEL 9

Why did Jezebel and Ahab have Naboth stoned to death?

a) because the Lord had commanded it
b) for his vineyard
c) to please those they ruled
d) because he preached against their marriage

Pages 342–345 Pages 354–357 Pages 366–369 Pages 378–381

Level 10

Charles Wesley uses the phrase "Sons of men and angels say" in which song?

a) "Christ the Lord Is Risen Today"
b) "Jesus Loves the Castaway"
c) "Rejoice, the Devil Is in Disarray"
d) "Love Divine, All Love Without Delay"

Level 11

In the song "Whispering Hope" by Alice Hawthorne (pseudonym of Septimus Winner), how is the voice of the angel described?

a) "hushed"
b) "soft"
c) "rejoicing"
d) "sweet"

Gold

Although he rejected labels, under what name did Watchman Nee's ministry become known?

a) Cottage Christian Movement
b) Little Flock Movement
c) Three Self Movement
d) Great Leap Forward

Pages 346–348 Pages 358–360 Pages 370–372 Pages 382–384

THIRTY INTERACTIVE QUIZZES THAT PUT YOU IN THE HOT SEAT

TRIVIA FOR LIFE

QUIZ 21

LEVEL 1

In William Cowper's song "There Is a Fountain," what fills the fountain?

a) "blood"
b) "balm"
c) "a healing stream"
d) "peace"

LEVEL 2

Whom was Paul talking about when he said, "Our dear friend, the doctor"?

a) Levi
b) Lydia
c) Luke
d) Lot

Pages 337–338 Pages 349–350 Pages 361–362 Pages 373–374

LEVEL 3

The greeting of "How do you do" is in which Albert E. Brumley song?

a) "Down in Memory Valley"
b) "I'll Meet You in the Morning"
c) "Turn Your Radio On"
d) "If We Never Meet Again"

BRONZE

In Leonardo da Vinci's *Last Supper,* what is Judas Iscariot holding?

a) a bag of money
b) an upside down cross
c) a dagger
d) a piece of bread

LEVEL 5

The unfinished fragments of Blaise Pascal's proposed book *Apology [Defense] of the Christian Religion* were published as what book?

a) *De la fréquente communion (Frequent Communion)*
b) *Pensées sur la religion (Thoughts on Religion)*
c) *L'honnêteté (Polite Respectability)*
d) *Lettres provinciales (Provincial Letters)*

Pages 339–341 Pages 351–353 Pages 363–365 Pages 375–377

LEVEL 6

What is the title of the Frances Ridley Havergal song with the words "consecrated, Lord, to Thee"?

a) "Is It for Me?"
b) "Another Year Is Dawning"
c) "Take My Life, and Let It Be"
d) "I Bring My Sins to Thee"

LEVEL 7

What word completes this statement by missionary martyr Jim Elliot: "He is no fool who gives what he cannot keep to gain what he cannot..."?

a) "see."
b) "lose."
c) "find."
d) "understand."

SILVER

Who wrote *Out of the Silent Planet,* a book that fused science fiction and religious allegory?

a) G. K. Chesterton
b) J. R. R. Tolkien
c) John Milton
d) C. S. Lewis

LEVEL 9

Hudson Taylor interrupted his work on what advanced degree to go to China?

a) Doctor of Fine Arts
b) Doctor of Medicine
c) Doctor of Divinity
d) Doctor of Music

Pages 342–345 Pages 354–357 Pages 366–369 Pages 378–381

Level 10

What is the title of Mahalia Jackson's autobiography?

a) *Movin' On*
b) *Queen of Gospel Song*
c) *We Shall Overcome*
d) *Hope Is the Hallmark*

Level 11

Besides keeping sheep, what did Amos of the Old Testament take care of before the Lord called him to prophesy?

a) a rich merchant's business
b) the king's stables
c) the tabernacle
d) sycamore-fig trees

Gold

Who was the founder of modern surgery who said, "I treated him; God healed him"?

a) Joseph Lister
b) William T. G. Morton
c) Louis Pasteur
d) Ambroise Paré

Pages 346–348 Pages 358–360 Pages 370–372 Pages 382–384

Quiz 22

Level 1

Martin Luther is considered the father of what upheaval?

a) Protestant Reformation
b) Great Awakening
c) Great Schism
d) German Renaissance

Level 2

What was the religious ministry of Dwight L. Moody?

a) upholding Genesis against secular humanism
b) serving as president of the Moody Bible Institute
c) evangelism
d) writing Bible commentaries

Pages 337–338 Pages 349–350 Pages 361–362 Pages 373–374

Level 3

What type of tree did John Chapman refer to in his lyrics, "I thank the Lord for giving me the sun and the rain and the. . ."?

a) "apple tree."
b) "family tree."
c) "tree of knowledge."
d) "tree of life."

Bronze

Which book by C. S. Lewis has Aslan, a Christlike character, in it?

a) *The Screwtape Letters*
b) *The Lion, the Witch and the Wardrobe*
c) *Surprised by Joy*
d) *Shadowlands*

Level 5

How could Billy Sunday's religious beliefs be described?

a) ecumenical
b) pentecostal
c) fundamental
d) liberal

Level 6

What did Jesus say as the widow gave two very small copper coins to the temple treasury?

a) "For with the measure you use, it will be measured to you."
b) "One coin would have been sufficient."
c) "It is hard for a rich person to enter the kingdom of heaven."
d) "This poor widow has put in more than all the others."

LEVEL 7

What color is associated with Lydia?

a) green
b) purple
c) blue
d) black

SILVER

What word completes the first line of Frances Ridley Havergal's song "True-hearted, whole-hearted, faithful and…"?

a) "glorious."
b) "loyal."
c) "regal."
d) "meek."

LEVEL 9

After Jacob kissed Rachel and began weeping aloud, what did she do?

a) said, "You are my own flesh and blood."
b) began to weep, too
c) gave him her family idols
d) ran and told her father, Laban

Pages 343–345 Pages 355–357 Pages 367–369 Pages 379–381

Level 10

What was one of Charles G. Finney's "new measures" for which he received criticism?

a) strict interpretation of predestination
b) the call for a public response to receive Christ after he finished preaching
c) refusal to allow public outbursts of emotion
d) preaching without singing or prayer

Level 11

How did Mahalia Jackson describe gospel music?

a) as songs of the sanctified church
b) as songs of fear and faith
c) as songs of the people
d) as songs of hope

Gold

What was Dwight L. Moody's first success as a Christian?

a) comforting soldiers during the Civil War
b) showing businessmen in England how to serve Jesus
c) preaching to prisoners at the Tombs in New York City
d) starting Sunday schools for slum children in Chicago

Pages 346–348 Pages 358–360 Pages 370–372 Pages 382–384

TRIVIA FOR LIFE

THIRTY INTERACTIVE QUIZZES THAT PUT YOU IN THE HOT SEAT

QUIZ 23

LEVEL 1

The words "Troublesome times are here, filling men's hearts with fear" are from what Robert E. Winsett song?

a) "The Message"
b) "Living by Faith"
c) "Jesus Is Coming Soon"
d) "Hallelujah! We Shall Rise"

LEVEL 2

What instrument is mentioned in the song "The King Is Coming" by Gloria Gaither, William J. Gaither, and Charles Milhuff?

a) cymbal
b) harp
c) lyre
d) trumpet

Pages 337–338 Pages 349–350 Pages 361–362 Pages 373–374

Level 3

Who is directly credited with writing thirty-seven of the Psalms and probably wrote many others?

a) David
b) Abraham
c) Moses
d) Solomon

Bronze

What phrase is found in the song "Send the Light" by Charles H. Gabriel?

a) "No clouds in heaven a shadow to cast"
b) "I'm pressing on the upward way"
c) "There are souls to rescue"
d) "O that will be glory"

Level 5

Which of the following worshipers of God could be described as a businesswoman?

a) Drusilla
b) Phoebe
c) Ruth
d) Lydia

Level 6

Why did Pocahontas (Matoaka) change her name to Rebecca?

a) English settlers found it easier to pronounce.
b) She took the name after becoming a Christian.
c) To pass for a European while in England.
d) So her father could not find her when she adopted English ways.

Pages 339–342 | Pages 351–354 | Pages 363–366 | Pages 375–378

Level 7

Who was the one who carried the news of the risen Lord to the disciples?

a) Rhoda
b) Mary of Bethany
c) Mary Magdalene
d) Mary the mother of Jesus

Silver

How did the four who carried the paralyzed man bring him before Jesus?

a) lowered him through an opening made in the roof
b) waited on the road to Jericho
c) lowered him in a basket from a sycamore-fig tree
d) waited for Jesus by a well

Level 9

Which songbook was written by Isaac Watts?

a) *Olney Hymns*
b) *Pocket Hymnbook for the Use of Christians of All Denominations*
c) *First Book of Songs or Ayres*
d) *Hymns and Spiritual Songs*

Pages 343–345 Pages 355–357 Pages 367–369 Pages 379–381

Level 10

What musical instrument did Miriam, Aaron's sister, play?

a) horn
b) harp
c) flute
d) tambourine

Level 11

The statement "For nothing is impossible with God" referred to what miracle?

a) salvation for the Gentiles
b) raising the dead
c) the virgin birth of Jesus
d) Elizabeth becoming a mother

Gold

In her best-known speech, what question did Sojourner Truth ask?

a) "Am I not a graduate from slavery with a diploma on my back?"
b) "How is it that we hear the loudest yelps for liberty from the drivers of slaves?"
c) "Ain't I a woman?"
d) "Did you do anything to lessen my load?"

Pages 346–348 Pages 358–360 Pages 370–372 Pages 382–384

QUIZ 24

LEVEL 1

How was John Newton first employed?

a) as a surveyor for the Liverpool shipyards
b) as a minister in Olney, England
c) as a gunpowder salesman
d) as a sailor engaged in slave trading

LEVEL 2

What did Jesus say to Peter in calling him as a disciple?

a) "The harvest is plentiful but the workers are few."
b) "It is not the healthy who need a doctor, but the sick."
c) "Go rather to the lost sheep of Israel."
d) "I will make you a fisher of men."

Pages 337–338 Pages 349–350 Pages 361–362 Pages 373–374

Level 3

Where did Amy Carmichael spend fifty-six years as a missionary?

a) China
b) Africa
c) India
d) Indonesia

Bronze

How did God react to Abel's offerings?

a) He said, "Your burnt offerings are not acceptable."
b) God spoke well of his offerings.
c) God didn't look with favor upon his offerings.
d) God sent out fire to consume the offerings.

Level 5

Of whom did Jesus say, "Among those born of women there has not risen anyone greater"?

a) Paul
b) Himself (Jesus)
c) John the Baptist
d) Lazarus

Level 6

What nickname is sometimes applied to Fanny J. Crosby?

a) Marching Matriarch
b) Wizard of Menlo Park
c) Swedish Nightingale
d) Hymn Queen

Pages 339–342 Pages 351–354 Pages 363–366 Pages 375–378

LEVEL 7

What happened to the widow of Zarephath after she supplied Elijah with food?

a) Her jar of flour was not used up, and the jug of oil did not run dry.
b) She was invited to eat at the king's table.
c) Twice as much was given to her.
d) She was restored to health.

SILVER

In Albert E. Brumley's hymn "I'll Fly Away," where is his home located?

a) "celestial shore"
b) "green valley"
c) "solid rock"
d) "inside a crystal palace"

LEVEL 9

What did Elisha have to do to receive a double portion of Elijah's spirit?

a) go upon a mountaintop to pray
b) cross over Jordan and preach in the next village
c) see Elijah as he was taken away
d) build an altar on Mount Carmel

Pages 343–345 Pages 355–357 Pages 367–369 Pages 379–381

Level 10

Albrecht Dürer's series of fifteen illustrations of the Apocalypse from Revelation was executed in what medium?

a) watercolor
b) woodcut
c) fresco
d) oil

Level 11

What is the subtitle of Sojourner Truth's autobiography, *The Narrative of Sojourner Truth:...*?

a) *I Lay My Burden Down*
b) *A Northern Slave*
c) *The Autobiography of a Female Slave*
d) *Scenes in the Life*

Gold

Who is called "the man of faith"?

a) Jacob
b) Isaac
c) Adam
d) Abraham

Pages 346–348 Pages 358–360 Pages 370–372 Pages 382–384

THIRTY INTERACTIVE QUIZZES THAT PUT YOU IN THE HOT SEAT

TRIVIA
FOR
LIFE

QUIZ 25

LEVEL 1

What practice of the church did Martin Luther oppose with his Ninety-five Theses?

a) the doctrine of transubstantiation of the Lord's Supper
b) the reliance upon tradition within the church
c) buying indulgences (the release from the penalties of sin)
d) the role of the pope

LEVEL 2

What two terms are associated with John Calvin's doctrine?

a) works and faith
b) conservatism and submission to authority
c) election and predestination
d) incarnation and atonement

Pages 337–338 Pages 349–350 Pages 361–362 Pages 373–374

LEVEL 3

For what is John Wycliffe noted?

a) building the first English printing press
b) first translation of the Bible into English
c) urging a closer tie between church and state
d) carrying Luther's reforms into England

BRONZE

What new believer did Barnabas introduce to the apostles in Jerusalem?

a) the Ethiopian
b) the jailer from Philippi
c) Paul, then known as Saul
d) Timothy

LEVEL 5

What did Brother Andrew (Andy van der Bijl) ask the Lord to do in his smuggler's prayer?

a) keep my car running
b) provide me a translator
c) put my foot in the door
d) make seeing eyes blind

LEVEL 6

What was the profession of Francis Scott Key, author of the United States national anthem?

a) lawyer
b) politician
c) sailor
d) businessman

Pages 339–342 Pages 351–354 Pages 363–366 Pages 375–378

Level 7

How did Billy Sunday describe a response to the gospel call?

a) hitting the sawdust trail
b) sliding into home
c) reclaiming your birthright
d) receiving honey from the rock

Silver

What do the songs "Joy to the World" and "Jesus Shall Reign Wher'er the Sun" by Isaac Watts have in common?

a) They were written after listening to sermons by John Calvin.
b) Martin Luther wrote the music.
c) Benjamin Franklin refused to publish them in America.
d) They are based on psalms in the Bible.

Level 9

When the children of Israel left slavery in Egypt, what happened to the bones of Joseph?

a) Pharaoh ordered that they be burned and scattered.
b) Moses took the bones with him.
c) Pharaoh's daughter secretly buried them.
d) They were lost forever.

Pages 343–345 Pages 355–357 Pages 367–369 Pages 379–381

Level 10

What ministry did Dawson Trotman found?

a) Youth with a Mission
b) The Navigators
c) Logos International
d) World Wide Pictures

Level 11

In addition to "kneel at the cross," what else does Charles E. Moody suggest in his song?

a) "lay every burden down"
b) "leave every care"
c) "dwell in Beulah Land"
d) "be covered with His blood"

Gold

Where did William Tyndale begin printing his translation of the Bible?

a) London, England
b) Hague, The Netherlands
c) Frankfurt, Germany
d) Cologne, Germany

Pages 346–348 Pages 358–360 Pages 370–372 Pages 382–384

QUIZ 26

LEVEL 1

In the Stuart K. Hines translation of the Swedish folk melody "How Great Thou Art," after he sees the stars, what does he hear?

a) "trumpet sound"
b) "thunder"
c) "whispering breezes"
d) "unseen footsteps"

LEVEL 2

In the Isaac Watts song "When I Survey the Wondrous Cross," what is poured on "my pride"?

a) "generous love"
b) "sorrows"
c) "wings of faith"
d) "contempt"

Pages 337–338 Pages 349–350 Pages 361–362 Pages 373–374

Level 3

For his work that began in Bristol, England, George Müller earned what title?

a) Poorest of the Poor
b) Bristol's Battling Minister
c) The Great Orator
d) Father of the Fatherless

Bronze

Mahalia Jackson is credited with bringing what music to a worldwide, multiracial audience?

a) ragtime
b) jazz
c) gospel
d) blues

Level 5

Because of Ezra's wisdom of God, what was he expected to do?

a) appoint magistrates and judges
b) coordinate rebuilding the walls of Jerusalem
c) make sure King Darius was happy
d) supervise the distribution of land inheritance

Level 6

Of what Scottish reformer did Mary, Queen of Scots, say, "I fear his prayers more than any army of ten thousand men"?

a) George Wishart
b) King James VI of Scotland
c) Thomas Chalmers
d) John Knox

Pages 339–342 Pages 351–354 Pages 363–366 Pages 375–378

Level 7

Complete the title of the Isaac Watts song: "O God, Our Help in. . . ."

a) "Times of Distress"
b) "Ages Past"
c) "Time of Need"
d) "Years to Come"

Silver

Doctor C. Everett Koop collaborated with Francis Schaeffer on what book and film series?

a) *The Flow of Biblical History*
b) *A Christian Manifesto*
c) *Whatever Happened to the Human Race?*
d) *No Final Conflict*

Level 9

Who was the pilot-missionary who died with Jim Elliot and the other missionaries in Ecuador?

a) Nate Saint
b) Johnny Angel
c) Russell Pastor
d) Reverend White

Pages 343–345 Pages 355–357 Pages 367–369 Pages 379–381

Level 10

What did Mary the mother of Jesus do after He ascended into heaven?

a) revisited the tomb where He was buried
b) went for a walk in the Garden of Gethsemane
c) went home to weep alone
d) went to an upstairs room with many others

Level 11

Which statement did William Tyndale make?

a) "The plowboy will know the scriptures better than the priests."
b) "It is impossible that any word of man should be equal with Holy Scriptures."
c) "We ought to believe in the authority of no man unless he says the word of God."
d) "You get the language from the common man in the marketplace."

Gold

Maltbie D. Babcock began his walks in the woods with what statement that later inspired a song?

a) "I'm going out to see my Father's world."
b) "I'm nearer home than I was yesterday."
c) "I'm stepping in the light."
d) "The path is long and steep."

Pages 346–348 Pages 358–360 Pages 370–372 Pages 382–384

THIRTY INTERACTIVE QUIZZES THAT PUT YOU IN THE HOT SEAT

TRIVIA FOR LIFE

Quiz 27

Level 1

What did George Bennard describe as "rugged" in his song?

a) a hillside
b) a ship of state
c) an old cross
d) the road to Jericho

Level 2

In his song, what did William Williams ask "Thou great Jehovah" to do?

a) "hide me"
b) "comfort me"
c) "guide me"
d) "show me"

Pages 337–338 Pages 349–350 Pages 361–362 Pages 373–374

Level 3

What is the first phrase in the song "He Touched Me" by William J. Gaither?

a) "Shackled by a heavy burden"
b) "There is strength"
c) "But praise God I belong"
d) "Come, Holy Spirit"

Bronze

The first stanza of the song "Silent Night" by Josef Mohr ends with what line?

a) "sleep in heavenly peace"
b) "round yon virgin mother and child"
c) "all is calm, all is bright"
d) "holy Infant so tender and mild"

Level 5

In the song "The Church in the Wildwood" by Dr. William S. Pitts, how does he describe the church?

a) "little brown church"
b) "log church"
c) "brick church"
d) "church with three bells"

Pages 339–341 Pages 351–353 Pages 363–365 Pages 375–377

Level 6

What line is found in the song "Low in the Grave He Lay," by Robert Lowry?

a) "nothing can for sin atone"
b) "my feeble faith looks up"
c) "O bless me now, my Savior"
d) "He arose a victor from the dark domain"

Level 7

Queen Esther risked her life by appearing unbidden before King Xerxes to press what worthy cause?

a) to remove the places of Baal worship
b) to prevent the killing of the Lord's prophets
c) to prevent the destruction of Jericho
d) to prevent the annihilation of the Jews

Silver

What career did Charles G. Finney leave to begin his Christian ministry?

a) lawyer
b) army officer
c) ship's captain
d) portrait painter

Level 9

When the Church of England pulpits were closed to him, what did John Wesley describe as his parish?

a) the Georgia Colony
b) the poor
c) the world
d) Europe

Pages 342–345 Pages 354–357 Pages 366–369 Pages 378–381

Level 10

Why did Charles Haddon Spurgeon withdraw from the Baptist Union?

a) its increasingly liberal attitude
b) it required a written examination to qualify for the ministry
c) it insisted that he preach against evolution
d) it refused to accept preachers of other denominations

Level 11

In Joseph Medlicott Scriven's song that has the words "all our sins and griefs to bear," how does he describe Jesus?

a) king
b) lover
c) friend
d) fortress

Gold

Why did Isaac Watts choose not to attend the University of Cambridge or Oxford?

a) He was so shy he could not leave home.
b) His grades were too poor.
c) He could not pay the tuition.
d) He was a Dissenter (Nonconformist).

Pages 346–348 Pages 358–360 Pages 370–372 Pages 382–384

QUIZ 28

LEVEL 1

The 1611 authorized English translation of the Bible was named for what person?

a) James I of England
b) Edgar Johnson Goodspeed
c) William Tyndale
d) Edward de Vere, 17th earl of Oxford

LEVEL 2

The statement "Here I stand, I cannot do otherwise" is attributed to whom?

a) Joan of Arc
b) Martin Luther
c) Galileo
d) Copernicus

Pages 337–338 Pages 349–350 Pages 361–362 Pages 373–374

Level 3

Although she repudiated it, what movie was based on the life of Gladys Aylward?

a) *China Diary*
b) *The Inn of the Sixth Happiness*
c) *The Sound of Music*
d) *The Good Earth*

Bronze

What was David Livingstone's term for slave trading in Africa?

a) a stranger's treasure
b) the open sore of the world
c) perpetual despotism
d) peculiar institution

Level 5

How does Gospel writer Luke describe Theophilus?

a) "Son of Encouragement"
b) "a man after his own heart"
c) "most excellent"
d) "Rabbi"

Pages 339–341 Pages 351–353 Pages 363–365 Pages 375–377

Level 6

How was Eunice related to Timothy?

a) cousin
b) sister
c) grandmother
d) mother

Level 7

My Utmost for His Highest by Oswald Chambers would best be described as what kind of book?

a) historical novel
b) religious allegory
c) devotional book
d) memoirs of a missionary

Silver

Who was the Christian believer who discovered the planet Uranus?

a) William Herschel
b) Ptolemy of Egypt
c) Jonathan Edwards
d) John Coach Adams

Level 9

In the Bible, who was the first woman mentioned by name after Eve?

a) Naamah, Tubal-Cain's sister
b) Adah, Lamech's wife
c) Milcah, Nahor's wife
d) Sarai or Sarah, Abraham's wife

x2 Pages 342–345 | Pages 354–357 | Pages 366–369 | Pages 378–381

LEVEL 10

The phrase "Teach me faith and duty" is from which Philip P. Bliss song?

a) "I Bring My Sins to Thee"
b) "More Holiness Give Me"
c) "Hallelujah! What a Savior!"
d) "Wonderful Words of Life"

LEVEL 11

How did Sojourner Truth's family become free?

a) as a result of the American Civil War
b) by a law of 1828 that freed slaves in New York State
c) by escaping to the North along the Underground Railroad
d) by being set free by their "owner"

GOLD

What grandmother does Paul describe as having a sincere faith?

a) Lois
b) Eunice
c) Tabitha
d) Priscilla

Pages 346–348 Pages 358–360 Pages 370–372 Pages 382–384

THIRTY INTERACTIVE QUIZZES THAT PUT YOU IN THE HOT SEAT

TRIVIA FOR LIFE

QUIZ 29

LEVEL 1

Paul is known as the apostle to what group?

a) twelve tribes of Israel
b) Hebrews
c) Gentiles
d) Macedonians

LEVEL 2

Who came to the empty tomb of Jesus while it was still dark?

a) Mary Magdalene
b) Herod
c) Peter
d) John

Pages 337–338 Pages 349–350 Pages 361–362 Pages 373–374

LEVEL 3

Noah was the first to see what phenomenon in the sky?

a) shooting star
b) rainbow
c) northern lights
d) comet

BRONZE

The words "And this be our motto, 'In God is our Trust'" are found in what song by Francis Scott Key?

a) "Star Spangled Banner"
b) "Hymn to the Flag"
c) "Hymn of the Patriots"
d) "God Save Our Beloved Country"

LEVEL 5

Teresa of Calcutta founded what organization?

a) Sisters of Our Lady of Loreto
b) Missionaries of Charity
c) People of the Pure Heart
d) City of Joy

Pages 339–341 Pages 351–353 Pages 363–365 Pages 375–377

LEVEL 6

What is a reasonable conclusion about Onesimus in Paul's letter to Philemon?

a) He was a runaway slave.
b) He was an army deserter.
c) He came from Caesar's household.
d) He was a silversmith.

LEVEL 7

What South American tribe made martyrs of Jim Elliot and four other missionary companions?

a) Auca
b) Carib
c) Maya
d) Tupi

SILVER

In addition to Joseph, who was Rachel's other son?

a) Levi
b) Benjamin
c) Reuben
d) Dan

LEVEL 9

What is the third book of the *Perelandra* trilogy by C. S. Lewis?

a) *Allegory of Love*
b) *Out of the Silent Planet*
c) *That Hideous Strength*
d) *The Last Battle*

Pages 342–345 Pages 354–357 Pages 366–369 Pages 378–381

Level 10

In his song, when does Andraé Crouch say, "We are going to see the King?"

a) "soon"
b) "when the roll is called up yonder"
c) "when the silver cord is broken"
d) "at the end of life's way"

Level 11

Henry Ward Beecher is noted primarily for which of his abilities?

a) organizer of missions
b) speaker
c) songwriter
d) writer

Gold

What was the title of William Carey's pamphlet that began the Baptist Missionary Movement?

a) *Enlarge the Place of Thy Tent*
b) *Expect Great Things from God; Attempt Great Things for God*
c) *Enquiry...to Use Means for the Conversion of the Heathens*
d) *The Urgent Duty of the Missionary Society*

Pages 346–348 Pages 358–360 Pages 370–372 Pages 382–384

Quiz 30

Level 1

What advice did hymn writer Horatio R. Palmer make part of the title of his song about temptation?

a) "pass over"
b) "go right"
c) "yield not"
d) "turn around"

Level 2

Jonathan Edwards is considered one of the evangelists who began what religious revival?

a) Renaissance
b) Protestant Reformation
c) American Enlightenment
d) Great Awakening

Pages 337–338 Pages 349–350 Pages 361–362 Pages 373–374

LEVEL 3

Although then known as separatists, Priscilla Mullins and the others aboard the *Mayflower* have become known by what name?

a) Old Comers
b) Leidenites
c) Pilgrims
d) Saints

BRONZE

How many times did Peter disown Jesus before the rooster crowed?

a) two
b) one
c) twelve
d) three

LEVEL 5

The song "Almost Persuaded" by Philip P. Bliss ends with what words?

a) "I am saved by the blood of the crucified one."
b) " 'Almost,' but lost!"
c) "Grace hath redeemed us once for all."
d) "Jesus loves even me."

LEVEL 6

Charles Haddon Spurgeon is noted for what aspect of his ministry?

a) his efforts to reconcile scripture and science
b) his preaching
c) his fund-raising
d) his establishment of a worldwide evangelistic association

Pages 339–342 Pages 351–354 Pages 363–366 Pages 375–378

Level 7

Hudson Taylor was the founder of what missionary organization?

a) Interdenominational Foreign Mission
b) China Inland Mission
c) Glad Tidings from England
d) China's Spiritual Need

Silver

Who was one of the prophets who appeared and talked with Jesus when He was transfigured?

a) Malachi
b) Gideon
c) Elisha
d) Elijah

Level 9

What phrase begins item 9 of the Dale Evans and Roy Rogers Riders Club Rules: "Love God and. . ."

a) "always obey your parents."
b) "go to Sunday school regularly."
c) "be kind to animals."
d) "consider others before yourself."

Pages 343–345 Pages 355–357 Pages 367–369 Pages 379–381

Level 10

Where did Ruth Bell, wife of Billy Graham, spend her youth?

a) Minneapolis, Minnesota
b) China and Korea
c) Montreat, North Carolina
d) Wheaton, Illinois

Level 11

Stephen's enemies hired men to say he had spoken against which Old Testament hero?

a) Aaron
b) Moses
c) David
d) Solomon

Gold

For how long did Charles Sheldon edit the *Daily Capital* newspaper of Topeka, Kansas, as he believed Jesus would have done?

a) one year
b) one month
c) one day
d) one week

Pages 346–348 Pages 358–360 Pages 370–372 Pages 382–384

Bonuses

Double Your Chances

Level 1

Incorrect answers include:

Quiz 1—B and D
Quiz 2—B and C
Quiz 3—A and D
Quiz 4—C and D
Quiz 5—B and C
Quiz 6—B and D
Quiz 7—B and D
Quiz 8—A and D
Quiz 9—B and D
Quiz 10—C and D
Quiz 11—A and C
Quiz 12—A and C
Quiz 13—C and D
Quiz 14—B and C
Quiz 15—B and C
Quiz 16—B and D
Quiz 17—A and B
Quiz 18—A and D
Quiz 19—A and C
Quiz 20—B and C
Quiz 21—B and D
Quiz 22—C and D
Quiz 23—A and B
Quiz 24—A and C
Quiz 25—A and D
Quiz 26—A and D
Quiz 27—A and D
Quiz 28—B and D
Quiz 29—A and D
Quiz 30—A and D

Double Your Chances

Level 2

Incorrect answers include:

Quiz 1—A and D
Quiz 2—A and C
Quiz 3—B and C
Quiz 4—A and D
Quiz 5—B and D
Quiz 6—B and D
Quiz 7—B and C
Quiz 8—C and D
Quiz 9—A and B
Quiz 10—A and D
Quiz 11—A and C
Quiz 12—A and D
Quiz 13—A and D
Quiz 14—A and D
Quiz 15—A and B
Quiz 16—B and D
Quiz 17—A and D
Quiz 18—A and D
Quiz 19—B and D
Quiz 20—A and B
Quiz 21—B and D
Quiz 22—B and D
Quiz 23—A and C
Quiz 24—A and B
Quiz 25—B and D
Quiz 26—A and C
Quiz 27—A and D
Quiz 28—A and D
Quiz 29—B and D
Quiz 30—B and C

Double Your Chances

Level 3

Incorrect Answers Include:

Quiz 1—B and C
Quiz 2—C and D
Quiz 3—C and D
Quiz 4—A and B
Quiz 5—A and B
Quiz 6—C and D
Quiz 7—C and D
Quiz 8—B and C
Quiz 9—B and D
Quiz 10—A and D
Quiz 11—B and C
Quiz 12—B and D
Quiz 13—A and B
Quiz 14—A and B
Quiz 15—A and C
Quiz 16—A and D
Quiz 17—A and B
Quiz 18—C and D
Quiz 19—A and C
Quiz 20—B and D
Quiz 21—C and D
Quiz 22—B and C
Quiz 23—C and D
Quiz 24—A and B
Quiz 25—A and C
Quiz 26—A and B
Quiz 27—B and C
Quiz 28—A and C
Quiz 29—C and D
Quiz 30—A and B

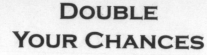

Double Your Chances

Bronze

Incorrect answers include:

Quiz 1—B and D
Quiz 2—A and D
Quiz 3—C and D
Quiz 4—A and D
Quiz 5—A and B
Quiz 6—B and C
Quiz 7—B and D
Quiz 8—C and D
Quiz 9—A and D
Quiz 10—A and C
Quiz 11—C and D
Quiz 12—C and D
Quiz 13—B and D
Quiz 14—A and C
Quiz 15—A and B
Quiz 16—A and C
Quiz 17—B and C
Quiz 18—C and D
Quiz 19—A and D
Quiz 20—A and B
Quiz 21—B and C
Quiz 22—C and D
Quiz 23—A and D
Quiz 24—A and C
Quiz 25—A and B
Quiz 26—B and D
Quiz 27—C and D
Quiz 28—C and D
Quiz 29—B and C
Quiz 30—A and B

Double Your Chances

Level 5

Incorrect answers include:

Quiz 1—B and C
Quiz 2—A and C
Quiz 3—C and D
Quiz 4—A and B
Quiz 5—B and C
Quiz 6—B and D
Quiz 7—B and C
Quiz 8—C and D
Quiz 9—B and D
Quiz 10—B and D
Quiz 11—C and D
Quiz 12—B and C
Quiz 13—B and D
Quiz 14—A and D
Quiz 15—A and B
Quiz 16—A and B
Quiz 17—C and D
Quiz 18—A and D
Quiz 19—C and D
Quiz 20—A and C
Quiz 21—A and C
Quiz 22—B and D
Quiz 23—B and C
Quiz 24—B and D
Quiz 25—A and C
Quiz 26—C and D
Quiz 27—C and D
Quiz 28—A and D
Quiz 29—C and D
Quiz 30—C and D

Double Your Chances

Level 6

Incorrect answers include:

Quiz 1—A and B
Quiz 2—C and D
Quiz 3—A and B
Quiz 4—A and C
Quiz 5—A and D
Quiz 6—B and D
Quiz 7—A and C
Quiz 8—C and D
Quiz 9—A and B
Quiz 10—C and D
Quiz 11—C and D
Quiz 12—A and C
Quiz 13—A and B
Quiz 14—A and C
Quiz 15—B and D
Quiz 16—B and C
Quiz 17—B and C
Quiz 18—B and C
Quiz 19—A and D
Quiz 20—A and B
Quiz 21—B and D
Quiz 22—A and B
Quiz 23—A and D
Quiz 24—A and B
Quiz 25—B and C
Quiz 26—B and C
Quiz 27—A and C
Quiz 28—B and C
Quiz 29—B and C
Quiz 30—C and D

Double Your Chances

Level 7

Incorrect answers include:

Quiz 1—B and D
Quiz 2—A and B
Quiz 3—A and C
Quiz 4—A and C
Quiz 5—A and D
Quiz 6—A and C
Quiz 7—C and D
Quiz 8—B and D
Quiz 9—B and D
Quiz 10—B and C
Quiz 11—A and B
Quiz 12—A and B
Quiz 13—B and C
Quiz 14—A and C
Quiz 15—C and D
Quiz 16—B and D
Quiz 17—A and D
Quiz 18—C and D
Quiz 19—A and D
Quiz 20—A and C
Quiz 21—A and C
Quiz 22—A and C
Quiz 23—A and B
Quiz 24—B and D
Quiz 25—B and C
Quiz 26—C and D
Quiz 27—B and C
Quiz 28—B and D
Quiz 29—B and C
Quiz 30—C and D

Double Your Chances

Silver

Incorrect answers include:

Quiz 1—C and D
Quiz 2—C and D
Quiz 3—C and D
Quiz 4—A and B
Quiz 5—B and C
Quiz 6—B and C
Quiz 7—A and D
Quiz 8—C and D
Quiz 9—C and D
Quiz 10—A and D
Quiz 11—A and C
Quiz 12—A and D
Quiz 13—A and C
Quiz 14—A and D
Quiz 15—B and D
Quiz 16—A and D
Quiz 17—B and D
Quiz 18—A and B
Quiz 19—A and B
Quiz 20—C and D
Quiz 21—B and C
Quiz 22—A and C
Quiz 23—B and C
Quiz 24—B and C
Quiz 25—A and C
Quiz 26—A and B
Quiz 27—C and D
Quiz 28—C and D
Quiz 29—C and D
Quiz 30—A and C

Double Your Chances

Level 9

Incorrect Answers Include:

Quiz 1—B and C
Quiz 2—B and C
Quiz 3—C and D
Quiz 4—B and D
Quiz 5—B and D
Quiz 6—B and C
Quiz 7—B and C
Quiz 8—B and D
Quiz 9—A and C
Quiz 10—A and C
Quiz 11—A and C
Quiz 12—C and D
Quiz 13—A and B
Quiz 14—B and C
Quiz 15—A and D
Quiz 16—A and C
Quiz 17—A and C
Quiz 18—A and D
Quiz 19—A and C
Quiz 20—A and D
Quiz 21—C and D
Quiz 22—B and C
Quiz 23—A and C
Quiz 24—B and D
Quiz 25—A and D
Quiz 26—B and D
Quiz 27—A and B
Quiz 28—A and C
Quiz 29—B and D
Quiz 30—A and C

Double Your Chances

Level 10

Incorrect answers include:

Quiz 1—B and D
Quiz 2—C and D
Quiz 3—B and C
Quiz 4—A and C
Quiz 5—B and D
Quiz 6—A and D
Quiz 7—A and C
Quiz 8—B and D
Quiz 9—C and D
Quiz 10—A and C
Quiz 11—C and D
Quiz 12—A and D
Quiz 13—C and D
Quiz 14—A and C
Quiz 15—A and B
Quiz 16—A and B
Quiz 17—B and D
Quiz 18—A and C
Quiz 19—C and D
Quiz 20—B and D
Quiz 21—B and C
Quiz 22—A and D
Quiz 23—A and C
Quiz 24—A and C
Quiz 25—C and D
Quiz 26—A and B
Quiz 27—B and C
Quiz 28—A and B
Quiz 29—B and C
Quiz 30—A and C

Double Your Chances

Level 11

Incorrect answers include:

Quiz 1—B and D
Quiz 2—C and D
Quiz 3—A and C
Quiz 4—A and B
Quiz 5—C and D
Quiz 6—A and C
Quiz 7—A and B
Quiz 8—B and D
Quiz 9—B and C
Quiz 10—B and D
Quiz 11—A and B
Quiz 12—A and D
Quiz 13—A and C
Quiz 14—B and D
Quiz 15—B and D
Quiz 16—A and D
Quiz 17—B and D
Quiz 18—B and C
Quiz 19—A and C
Quiz 20—C and D
Quiz 21—A and C
Quiz 22—B and C
Quiz 23—A and B
Quiz 24—C and D
Quiz 25—A and D
Quiz 26—B and D
Quiz 27—A and B
Quiz 28—A and C
Quiz 29—A and D
Quiz 30—A and D

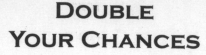

Double Your Chances

Gold

Incorrect answers include:

Quiz 1—B and C
Quiz 2—A and C
Quiz 3—B and D
Quiz 4—A and C
Quiz 5—A and C
Quiz 6—C and D
Quiz 7—B and C
Quiz 8—B and D
Quiz 9—A and B
Quiz 10—C and D
Quiz 11—B and D
Quiz 12—A and C
Quiz 13—A and C
Quiz 14—A and D
Quiz 15—A and C
Quiz 16—C and D
Quiz 17—B and C
Quiz 18—A and D
Quiz 19—B and C
Quiz 20—A and C
Quiz 21—A and C
Quiz 22—A and B
Quiz 23—B and D
Quiz 24—B and C
Quiz 25—A and C
Quiz 26—B and D
Quiz 27—A and C
Quiz 28—B and C
Quiz 29—B and D
Quiz 30—A and B

Have a Hint

Level 1

Quiz 1—Also known as the Book of Books.
Quiz 2—As in "_____ Bless America."
Quiz 3—A telephone you dial yourself without an operator.
Quiz 4—Short song, short name.
Quiz 5—Not a pellet of medication to be taken internally.
Quiz 6—Zero, zilch, nada, goose egg.
Quiz 7—A bookcase hid the entrance.
Quiz 8—For a special effect, mix red food color and syrup.
Quiz 9—Like Carl Sandburg's fog...
Quiz 10—Opposite the agony of defeat.
Quiz 11—Platform divers sometimes do only half of one.
Quiz 12—I don't know the words, but I can hum a few bars.
Quiz 13—Bermuda has a triangle and Wyoming has a tower.
Quiz 14—A visitor "not of this world."
Quiz 15—Think "from Stettin in the Baltic to Trieste in the Adriatic."
Quiz 16—Camouflaged to conceal an identity.
Quiz 17—Yellowstone's best-known geyser.
Quiz 18—But it's not about Ben-Hur.
Quiz 19—The first three letters are a transgression of the Ten Commandments.
Quiz 20—Heroism ends with the same letters.
Quiz 21—Is it O positive or B negative?
Quiz 22—When change failed, opposition followed.
Quiz 23—Pronto...
Quiz 24—Subject of Lincoln's proclamation of 1863.
Quiz 25—Follow the money.
Quiz 26—Sound from a lightning discharge.
Quiz 27—You can do this to your fingers and your heart.
Quiz 28—He also had a "town" in Virginia.
Quiz 29—The word comes from "gentle."
Quiz 30—In both the United States and Europe, this traffic sign is triangular.

Have a Hint

Level 2

Quiz 1—Hallelujah has the same meaning.
Quiz 2—A government worker: civil ____.
Quiz 3—In Arab countries, the flag has a scarlet crescent.
Quiz 4—Aaron could be described as "silver tongued."
Quiz 5—Originally, military expeditions to the Holy Land.
Quiz 6—Abraham Lincoln was born in one.
Quiz 7—What Columbus sought by sailing west.
Quiz 8—The EKG is not a flat line.
Quiz 9—Home of cheese and chocolate.
Quiz 10—Bracelets with the letters WWJD summarize the question.
Quiz 11—It has twenty-eight bones.
Quiz 12—It's a wind instrument.
Quiz 13—Without insects, life itself is impossible.
Quiz 14—Did he also name the projection at the front of your throat?
Quiz 15—George Washington could have said the same about Benedict Arnold.
Quiz 16—It's similar to the title of Dickens's book that begins "It was the best of times, it was the worse of times."
Quiz 17—She often made the final bed check of injured soldiers well after dark.
Quiz 18—The coronation of 1952 gave Great Britain a queen of the same name.
Quiz 19—What a gentleman offered a lady as she stepped from a coach.
Quiz 20—They sought a disciplined method of spiritual improvement.
Quiz 21—The name is Lucas in Latin.
Quiz 22—Short answer...
Quiz 23—An instrument to announce the arrival of a king.
Quiz 24—Think about the elderly Cuban in Hemingway's short novel.
Quiz 25—The first Tuesday after the first Monday in November in the United States.
Quiz 26—Disrespect in court...
Quiz 27—A Seeing Eye dog.
Quiz 28—Comic duo Dean _____ and Jerry Lewis.
Quiz 29—M & M, but not candy.
Quiz 30—What bears do in spring.

HAVE A HINT

LEVEL 3

Quiz 1—The first name of the president from Quincy, Massachusetts.
Quiz 2—Moisture-laden fragrant flowers with prickly stems.
Quiz 3—Because of the height, it took an "angel" to paint it.
Quiz 4—The eatable parts grow underground.
Quiz 5—"Walk a mile in them…"
Quiz 6—Look before you leap…
Quiz 7—The fourth Thursday in November.
Quiz 8—Native American Nez Percé leader Chief ____.
Quiz 9—It would take a maternity maturity ward.
Quiz 10—Reach out and _____ somebody.
Quiz 11—Neither fig nor Wayne.
Quiz 12—The U.S. Navy's military police are known as the _____ patrol.
Quiz 13—Its official publication is "The War Cry."
Quiz 14—Think carpus and phalanges.
Quiz 15—Splendor to the infant monarch.
Quiz 16—A female parent.
Quiz 17—Take the first letter of Jesus, others, yourself.
Quiz 18—Charles Dickens's character: _____ Copperfield.
Quiz 19—Knights wore shining metallic suits.
Quiz 20—He wore white socks in Chicago.
Quiz 21—A twining vine: the _____ glory.
Quiz 22—What would Johnny Appleseed sing about?
Quiz 23—He showed Goliath his skill with a slingshot.
Quiz 24—Columbus named Native Americans for this destination.
Quiz 25—Two hundred years before the King James Version.
Quiz 26—More than genes are required to be one.
Quiz 27—How Harry Houdini was restrained.
Quiz 28—The number was reduced from eight.
Quiz 29—Roy G Biv tells the order of the colors.
Quiz 30—John Wayne: "Well, listen, ____."

Have a Hint

Bronze

Quiz 1—John Philip Sousa music.
Quiz 2—A fraternal question.
Quiz 3—One of Satan's henchmen for each of the seven deadly sins.
Quiz 4—Think double w.
Quiz 5—Did they change color in the fall?
Quiz 6—Jesus spoke the beatitudes from such a location.
Quiz 7—Six-foot six-inch basketball player Michael ______.
Quiz 8—A tourniquet stems the flow.
Quiz 9—CPR for the soul.
Quiz 10—We try to keep these; He is certain to.
Quiz 11—A global worry...
Quiz 12—Usually portrayed as a limbless reptile.
Quiz 13—Fungi can do without it.
Quiz 14—If Peter had a sister, so would Andrew.
Quiz 15—Homer and Milton would have been in good company with her.
Quiz 16—Little Bo Peep had a similar occupation.
Quiz 17—Antique enemy...
Quiz 18—Judy Garland's St. Louis World's Fair movie.
Quiz 19—Vertigo...
Quiz 20—George Orwell's *Animal Farm* is one of the few modern examples.
Quiz 21—You'd find one in a Brinks armored truck.
Quiz 22—A place for clothes.
Quiz 23—SOS would be appropriate.
Quiz 24—Abel got an "atta boy."
Quiz 25—Did he suggest the name change?
Quiz 26—Jerry Falwell's television broadcast, the "Old Time ______ Hour."
Quiz 27—A newborn does it for about 16 hours a day.
Quiz 28—Unobstructed skin lesion of the human habitation.
Quiz 29—He wrote it by the rockets' red glare.
Quiz 30—Subtract four from the number of days in the week.

Have a Hint

Level 5

Quiz 1—Alms for the poor.
Quiz 2—He prevented Southern forces from capturing Washington, D.C., during the Civil War.
Quiz 3—They have trumpet-shaped flowers.
Quiz 4—They were sad, you see.
Quiz 5—Don't tell the NFL.
Quiz 6—The name rhymes with macaroni.
Quiz 7—The family name would survive.
Quiz 8—A dove carrying an olive branch...
Quiz 9—The original Nick at Nite.
Quiz 10—The Charge of the Light Brigade was a "crime."
Quiz 11—He had a lot of time on his hands.
Quiz 12—According to Noel Coward, only mad dogs and Englishmen go out in its noonday sun.
Quiz 13—London's West End manors had these both upstairs and downstairs.
Quiz 14—Soldiers met in battle wearing blue and gray.
Quiz 15—The only one known by three names.
Quiz 16—Vegetarians need not apply.
Quiz 17—They are usually shown with wings and a harp.
Quiz 18—Pronounce his name differently for a task to be done.
Quiz 19—Good things come in threes.
Quiz 20—The inscription on his crypt in a church reads, "If you seek his monument, look around."
Quiz 21—He engaged his little gray cells.
Quiz 22—Back to basics...
Quiz 23—Anagram: Daily.
Quiz 24—Attila the Hun and Peter the Great had the same middle name.
Quiz 25—Like a guide dog with a white cane.
Quiz 26—They have power to enforce the law.
Quiz 27—A drab color.
Quiz 28—Equivalent to a grade of A plus.
Quiz 29—It follows Lincoln's statement that begins "with malice toward none..."
Quiz 30—Only in horseshoes can falling short count.

Have a Hint

Level 6

Quiz 1—The Nile runs through it.
Quiz 2—Two pairs of double letters.
Quiz 3—One was the child of the other's uncle.
Quiz 4—Number of islands in the salad dressing.
Quiz 5—She was taking a "bath" when David saw her.
Quiz 6—The same complaint is made of drivers who use cell phones.
Quiz 7—He wrote a book defending writing in the vernacular.
Quiz 8—He needed skill at the first of the three Rs.
Quiz 9—Sounds like water at 212 degrees Fahrenheit.
Quiz 10—Ships would prefer it during stormy weather.
Quiz 11—Think "good" about a citizen from there.
Quiz 12—He developed the process to keep milk from spoiling.
Quiz 13—If the meaning of her name matched her disposition, she had a rosy outlook.
Quiz 14—When he did, Jesus gained another disciple.
Quiz 15—No strings attached. . .
Quiz 16—His enemies wanted him dead, dead.
Quiz 17—Consider Robert Stroud's feathered subjects of study at Alcatraz.
Quiz 18—His given name is the same as Princess Diana's oldest son.
Quiz 19—Consider the third inalienable right of the Declaration of Independence.
Quiz 20—Batteries not included.
Quiz 21—Last words are the title to the Beatles' last album.
Quiz 22—It's not the gift but the thought that counts.
Quiz 23—A new name after being "born again."
Quiz 24—She wrote about six thousand songbook entries.
Quiz 25—Dick the butcher of Shakespeare's *Henry VI:* "First you kill the _____."
Quiz 26—Append "ville" for a city in Tennessee.
Quiz 27—Opposite of the agony of defeat.
Quiz 28—Today, he would telephone her on the second Sunday in May.
Quiz 29—No Underground Railroad for him.
Quiz 30—His sermons filled fifty volumes.

Have a Hint

Level 7

Quiz 1—An "old-fashioned gospel" preacher.
Quiz 2—When she died, the destitute missed her.
Quiz 3—Think Demosthenes and Daniel Webster.
Quiz 4—The wrong name on the wanted poster.
Quiz 5—What a hospice volunteer does.
Quiz 6—Where the ball goes when the announcer says, "He shoots, he scores!"
Quiz 7—Always the paperwork...
Quiz 8—Roget would say the "municipality of ruin."
Quiz 9—They warn of treacherous coastal waters.
Quiz 10—The people of Plymouth Colony.
Quiz 11—Espionage is not for the faint of heart.
Quiz 12—The original "hush puppy" food.
Quiz 13—Last word is decorative iron.
Quiz 14—He began at the beginning.
Quiz 15—Charlton Heston parted the Red Sea in this role.
Quiz 16—Opposite of a dirty devil.
Quiz 17—A major city together with its suburbs.
Quiz 18—Think days ahead and times before.
Quiz 19—Words of single syllables.
Quiz 20—Pioneer television comic _____ Berle.
Quiz 21—Often quoted as "give," Nathan Hale instead used this word in his last statement.
Quiz 22—Steven Spielberg's movie with Oprah Winfrey had the same color in the title.
Quiz 23—She was probably from the town of Magdala.
Quiz 24—The original "all you care to eat" buffet.
Quiz 25—Was it a "beaten" path?
Quiz 26—It's the time frame of archaeology.
Quiz 27—A BC holocaust in the making.
Quiz 28—Take a daily vitamin for the human spirit.
Quiz 29—The first alphabetically.
Quiz 30—In case of a typhoon, it's a good location.

Have a Hint

Silver

Quiz 1—Fingertips to fingertips...
Quiz 2—Hydrotherapy...
Quiz 3—His price was twenty shekels of silver.
Quiz 4—The number of angles in a triangle.
Quiz 5—A highly contagious disease.
Quiz 6—The germ killer Listerine was named in his honor.
Quiz 7—To be politically correct, person.
Quiz 8—Marco Polo saw this practice that gave Chinese women dainty appearances.
Quiz 9—Pulp and historical are cousins of this genre.
Quiz 10—Columbus's flagship carried the same name.
Quiz 11—But Paul was bound and determined to go to Jerusalem.
Quiz 12—Henry Morton Stanley said, "Dr. ____, I presume."
Quiz 13—She had four times the experience of a twenty-one year old.
Quiz 14—The watcher was a female sibling.
Quiz 15—A whodunit...
Quiz 16—He traveled with a container of bread and fruit of the vine.
Quiz 17—Think generous patrons...
Quiz 18—Meet one in an ER...
Quiz 19—I'm all ears.
Quiz 20—When opportunity knocks, let it in.
Quiz 21—William Clark's partner in the "Corps of Discovery."
Quiz 22—Greyfriars Bobby, the dog, had this attribute.
Quiz 23—Did the homeowner's insurance repair the damage?
Quiz 24—A heavenly beach.
Quiz 25—Paraphrased scripture.
Quiz 26—They were not talking about the 100m dash.
Quiz 27—Marshall Matt Dillon brought ______ and order to Dodge City.
Quiz 28—Last name begins with feminine pronoun.
Quiz 29—The first name of the American who flew a kite during a lightning storm.
Quiz 30—Every other letter is a vowel.

Have a Hint

Level 9

Quiz 1—Could their fleece be white as snow?
Quiz 2—As a youth, Whitefield had been interested in acting and theater.
Quiz 3—"We shall overcome" for females.
Quiz 4—The reason Jack and Jill went up the hill.
Quiz 5—The buddy system.
Quiz 6—Shorthand came in handy.
Quiz 7—A quarter of a year.
Quiz 8—Squash begins with the letters of the name.
Quiz 9—To sketch with a pencil.
Quiz 10—Jefferson's land deal, the Louisiana _____.
Quiz 11—"___ is believing."
Quiz 12—He wore a queue.
Quiz 13—The Gestapo tried to force Bonhoeffer to ____ crimes against Hitler.
Quiz 14—The first name of Simon who met the pie man.
Quiz 15—The wrong kind puffeth up.
Quiz 16—It means a petition.
Quiz 17—It is more than the absence of war.
Quiz 18—Although in his day the term "Indians" was used.
Quiz 19—She was a judge and ruled Israel.
Quiz 20—Vegetables would grow there, too.
Quiz 21—Later, he completed the studies and took the Hippocratic oath.
Quiz 22—And it wasn't even the third Sunday in June.
Quiz 23—The only one with "spirit."
Quiz 24—He needed the motto of the Pinkertons: We never sleep.
Quiz 25—They crossed the Red Sea, too.
Quiz 26—Think rhyming...
Quiz 27—The 1900s had two wars named after the correct choice.
Quiz 28—After adage and before Adam in the dictionary.
Quiz 29—The Olympic event "clean and jerk" requires this.
Quiz 30—Dress in your best...

Have a Hint

Level 10

Quiz 1—Canada geese migrate more quickly with its help.
Quiz 2—The sun does it each morning.
Quiz 3—For Bonhoeffer it became the cost of living.
Quiz 4—Native American moon. . .
Quiz 5—Participants do this in the Olympic marathon.
Quiz 6—Consider his wife's first name: Joy.
Quiz 7—It wasn't because of a migraine.
Quiz 8—No need to carry credit cards.
Quiz 9—First word is a woman's name.
Quiz 10—Reading and 'riting and 'rithmetic. . .
Quiz 11—A college professor has a similar job.
Quiz 12—He couldn't sleep or concentrate; he felt sad.
Quiz 13—He said "aye, aye, sir" to God.
Quiz 14—What happens when a long and boring sermon ends.
Quiz 15—The flower _____'s Ladder is named for one of his dreams.
Quiz 16—Think divine blueprints.
Quiz 17—The female of the species.
Quiz 18—Cartoon, a boy and his tiger: "_____ and Hobbs."
Quiz 19—A believer's alias.
Quiz 20—Ends with morning network TV news show. . .
Quiz 21—The ending "g" is dropped.
Quiz 22—Like Bob Barker, he said, "Come on down!"
Quiz 23—It is a percussion instrument.
Quiz 24—Extra copies were "a chip off the old block."
Quiz 25—Compass and sextant. . .
Quiz 26—She did not have an elevator to get there.
Quiz 27—A college degree for a nonscientist is called a _____ arts degree.
Quiz 28—It shares words with the Jimmy Stewart classic Christmas movie: *It's a* _____ _____.
Quiz 29—Participants in the Oklahoma Land Rush. . .
Quiz 30—Home of the Great Wall.

Have a Hint

Level 11

Quiz 1—The number of strikes in an out.
Quiz 2—Brothers told him to "Go west, young man."
Quiz 3—A young man of great physical beauty?
Quiz 4—A generous titan of industry.
Quiz 5—They could say, "Here comes the judge!"
Quiz 6—Hans Anderson's middle name.
Quiz 7—Life insurance companies could not do without it.
Quiz 8—The umpire calls the ball "low and _____."
Quiz 9—Her first name is the city of her birth in this country.
Quiz 10—A word that is used to ask permission of a court.
Quiz 11—Ends with the worldwide staple cereal grain.
Quiz 12—A Sanskrit version of the Rosetta stone would have helped.
Quiz 13—Look for the "no" in the middle of the name.
Quiz 14—Preacher to the Western Hemisphere south of the United States.
Quiz 15—The material world...
Quiz 16—Life, liberty, and the _____ of happiness.
Quiz 17—Consider Bobbie Gentry's song "_____ Valley PTA."
Quiz 18—A hilarious joke should earn the same response.
Quiz 19—You can't take the pass book with you.
Quiz 20—Tissues are advertised as having this property.
Quiz 21—A cookie named after Newton.
Quiz 22—Former President Clinton's hometown in Arkansas.
Quiz 23—She was barren and beyond childbearing years.
Quiz 24—A slave on the New York side of the Mason-Dixon Line.
Quiz 25—Abandon worries without exception.
Quiz 26—He would be turning over the soil in the spring.
Quiz 27—A Quaker might agree.
Quiz 28—The state acted before the federal government.
Quiz 29—Patrick Henry and William Jennings Bryan also held people's attention with this skill.
Quiz 30—Often portrayed holding two stone tablets.

Have a Hint

Gold

Quiz 1—To play the role in a movie, women need not apply.
Quiz 2—Phototropic plants do it when the sun is overhead.
Quiz 3—She was known as Amma, meaning "mother" in the Tamil language.
Quiz 4—Countryman to Sir Walter Scott and Robert Louis Stevenson.
Quiz 5—Shares a name with the scientist Asimov.
Quiz 6—Romulus and Remus, Castor and Pollux...
Quiz 7—Although it is not likely that she was led around by it.
Quiz 8—The planet Venus is also known by this name.
Quiz 9—Migrating Canada geese do it.
Quiz 10—He is not related to the big-band leader.
Quiz 11—Not the coffee.
Quiz 12—A victim of Hitler's executioners.
Quiz 13—A place to stay during an alpine blizzard.
Quiz 14—Despite coming up from bondage, he wrote with eloquence and brilliance.
Quiz 15—And they were not referring to the black clover of a playing card.
Quiz 16—The thrill of victory...
Quiz 17—Who could find first name "Brother" last name "Andrew"?
Quiz 18—Also known as a domestic.
Quiz 19—Probably not the result of a potato fungus.
Quiz 20—Gaggle and pride are similar names.
Quiz 21—In English, his last name means to remove with a knife.
Quiz 22—He arranged pony rides and picnics for them.
Quiz 23—A contraction of "am not."
Quiz 24—The sixteenth U.S. president's first name.
Quiz 25—Also the home of the men's fragrance.
Quiz 26—God's terrestrial sphere.
Quiz 27—A minority opinion...
Quiz 28—There is no "t" in this name.
Quiz 29—Those who did not acknowledge the God of Abraham.
Quiz 30—Seven days without God makes one weak.

Look in the Book

Level 1

Quiz 1—2 Timothy 3:16
Quiz 2—Ephesians 4:6
Quiz 3—Ephesians 2:18
Quiz 4—Matthew 1:21
Quiz 5—Luke 1:63
Quiz 6—Exodus 9:6
Quiz 7—Matthew 6:6
Quiz 8—1 Chronicles 22:8
Quiz 9—Genesis 34:3
Quiz 10—1 Corinthians 15:55
Quiz 11—Philippians 1:21
Quiz 12—Romans 15:9
Quiz 13—Matthew 4:1
Quiz 14—Matthew 1:20
Quiz 15—Hebrews 9:3
Quiz 16—Genesis 38:14
Quiz 17—Romans 1:17
Quiz 18—2 Kings 6:17
Quiz 19—Exodus 34:29
Quiz 20—Acts 21:8
Quiz 21—John 19:34
Quiz 22—Jeremiah 26:13
Quiz 23—Revelation 22:20
Quiz 24—1 Timothy 1:10
Quiz 25—Acts 8:20
Quiz 26—Psalm 77:18
Quiz 27—Philippians 2:8
Quiz 28—Acts 15:13
Quiz 29—Galatians 2:8
Quiz 30—Deuteronomy 13:8

Look in the Book

Level 2

Quiz 1—Romans 15:11
Quiz 2—Luke 1:38
Quiz 3—Colossians 1:20
Quiz 4—Exodus 4:14–16
Quiz 5—Mark 15:13 begins with first three letters
Quiz 6—1 Chronicles 27:32
Quiz 7—Mark 16:1
Quiz 8—John 14:19
Quiz 9—Matthew 27:45 ends with last word
Quiz 10—Mark 10:51
Quiz 11—Acts 7:50
Quiz 12—1 Thessalonians 4:16
Quiz 13—Matthew 3:4
Quiz 14—Genesis 2:19
Quiz 15—Mark 14:18
Quiz 16—Mark 1:1
Quiz 17—Mark 4:21
Quiz 18—Luke 1:24
Quiz 19—Psalm 18:35
Quiz 20—Ruth 4:7
Quiz 21—Colossians 4:14
Quiz 22—Ephesians 4:11
Quiz 23—Matthew 24:31
Quiz 24—Matthew 4:19
Quiz 25—2 Peter 1:10
Quiz 26—1 Thessalonians 5:20
Quiz 27—Psalm 43:3
Quiz 28—Revelation 3:16 word 5, first two letters + word 6, last four letters
Quiz 29—John 20:1
Quiz 30—Isaiah 52:1

Look in the Book

Level 3

Quiz 1—John 1:1
Quiz 2—Job 38:28
Quiz 3—Jude 1:9
Quiz 4—Judges 14:14
Quiz 5—Mark 1:7
Quiz 6—Acts 27:43
Quiz 7—1 Timothy 4:4
Quiz 8—Matthew 1:5–16
Quiz 9—John 3:4
Quiz 10—Luke 8:44
Quiz 11—Hebrews 11:20
Quiz 12—John 6:1
Quiz 13—Titus 2:11
Quiz 14—Ecclesiastes 5:6
Quiz 15—Luke 2:14
Quiz 16—Genesis 17:16
Quiz 17—John 17:13
Quiz 18—Psalm 23:4
Quiz 19—Ephesians 6:13
Quiz 20—Isaiah 22:18
Quiz 21—1 Samuel 15:12
Quiz 22—Song of Songs 2:3
Quiz 23—Psalm 3
Quiz 24—Esther 1:1
Quiz 25—Ezra 4:18
Quiz 26—Psalm 68:5
Quiz 27—Deuteronomy 1:9
Quiz 28—Matthew 20:5
Quiz 29—Genesis 9:13
Quiz 30—Anagram: Genesis 24:16 second word + Psalm 119:130 first four letters of last word

Look in the Book

Bronze

Quiz 1—1 Peter 2:6
Quiz 2—Genesis 4:9
Quiz 3—Mark 16:9
Quiz 4—John 5:17
Quiz 5—Genesis 3:7
Quiz 6—Isaiah 13:2
Quiz 7—Matthew 3:5
Quiz 8—Mark 10:45
Quiz 9—Psalm 85:6
Quiz 10—Psalm 106:12
Quiz 11—Genesis 11:1
Quiz 12—Genesis 3:15
Quiz 13—Job 8:16
Quiz 14—John 1:40
Quiz 15—Acts 9:9
Quiz 16—Genesis 4:2
Quiz 17—Psalm 61:3
Quiz 18—2 Kings 6:1
Quiz 19—Acts 19:32
Quiz 20—Ezekiel 17:2
Quiz 21—John 13:29
Quiz 22—Proverbs 30:30
Quiz 23—Psalm 69:18
Quiz 24—Hebrews 11:4
Quiz 25—Acts 9:27
Quiz 26—Mark 13:10
Quiz 27—Psalm 4:8
Quiz 28—Isaiah 1:6
Quiz 29—Matthew 2:10
Quiz 30—Matthew 26:75

LOOK IN THE BOOK

LEVEL 5

Quiz 1—Mark 10:46
Quiz 2—Mark 6:21
Quiz 3—Matthew 6:28
Quiz 4—Matthew 3:7
Quiz 5—Acts 20:7
Quiz 6—Ruth 1:15–16
Quiz 7—Luke 7:15
Quiz 8—Jude 1:2
Quiz 9—John 3:1–2
Quiz 10—2 Samuel 8:6
Quiz 11—Acts 5:18
Quiz 12—Esther 1:1
Quiz 13—Psalm 123:2
Quiz 14—2 Timothy 2:4
Quiz 15—Luke 13:34 first four letters of last word
Quiz 16—Acts 10:12–13
Quiz 17—Acts 27:23
Quiz 18—Job 1:8
Quiz 19—Deuteronomy 19:9
Quiz 20—Hebrews 11:10
Quiz 21—1 Corinthians 3:20
Quiz 22—Acts 2:13 fourth word begins correct answer
Quiz 23—Acts 16:14
Quiz 24—Matthew 11:11
Quiz 25—John 12:40
Quiz 26—Ezra 7:25
Quiz 27—Zechariah 1:8
Quiz 28—Luke 1:3
Quiz 29—1 Corinthians 13:13 (KJV)
Quiz 30—Psalm 73:2

Look in the Book

Level 6

Quiz 1—Matthew 2:13
Quiz 2—Ecclesiastes 10:10
Quiz 3—Esther 2:7
Quiz 4—1 Corinthians 14:19
Quiz 5—Matthew 1:6
Quiz 6—Luke 10:40
Quiz 7—Genesis 11:1
Quiz 8—Acts 8:30
Quiz 9—Ezekiel 24:5 sounds like word 18
Quiz 10—Luke 23:37
Quiz 11—Luke 17:15–16
Quiz 12—John 10:9 sounds like last word
Quiz 13—Acts 12:13–14
Quiz 14—John 1:41
Quiz 15—Psalm 54:6
Quiz 16—Numbers 31:10
Quiz 17—Acts 16:26
Quiz 18—Leviticus 16:22 words 3 and 4, sounds like
Quiz 19—1 Timothy 2:15
Quiz 20—1 Peter 1:1 starts with word 9
Quiz 21—Psalm 119:109
Quiz 22—Luke 21:3
Quiz 23—Acts 11:26
Quiz 24—Mark 14:26
Quiz 25—Titus 3:13
Quiz 26—Revelation 1:1
Quiz 27—1 Corinthians 15:57
Quiz 28—2 Timothy 1:5
Quiz 29—Philemon 1:16
Quiz 30—2 Peter 2:5

Look in the Book

Level 7

Quiz 1—1 Timothy 4:16
Quiz 2—Acts 9:36
Quiz 3—Acts 4:29
Quiz 4—Nehemiah 6:11
Quiz 5—Luke 10:34
Quiz 6—Acts 9:25
Quiz 7—Ecclesiastes 10:5
Quiz 8—Isaiah 19:18
Quiz 9—Isaiah 2:5
Quiz 10—Matthew 23:15
Quiz 11—Judges 9:31
Quiz 12—Matthew 15:27
Quiz 13—Numbers 23:23 (KJV)
Quiz 14—Genesis 1:1
Quiz 15—Exodus 2:19–21
Quiz 16—Revelation 22:16
Quiz 17—Acts 7:45
Quiz 18—Exodus 8:10
Quiz 19—Daniel 2:28
Quiz 20—Luke 3:15 words 14 and 15 first two letters
Quiz 21—Luke 9:25
Quiz 22—Acts 16:14
Quiz 23—John 20:18
Quiz 24—1 Kings 17:14
Quiz 25—Matthew 7:3
Quiz 26—Ephesians 3:9
Quiz 27—Esther 7:4
Quiz 28—Acts 2:42
Quiz 29—Luke 2:1 rearrange first two letters of Roman ruler title and name
Quiz 30—Acts 1:17

Look in the Book

Silver

Quiz 1—1 Timothy 2:8
Quiz 2—Psalm 42:1
Quiz 3—Genesis 37:28
Quiz 4—Genesis 4:25
Quiz 5—Deuteronomy 25: 14 last word
Quiz 6—Acts 11:27 starts with letters of last word
Quiz 7—1 Corinthians 2:15
Quiz 8—Luke 7:46
Quiz 9—1 Thessalonians 1:3
Quiz 10—Acts 27:6
Quiz 11—Acts 21:11
Quiz 12—1 Peter 2:5 words 4 and 5
Quiz 13—Luke 2:37
Quiz 14—Exodus 2:4
Quiz 15—Ephesians 5:32
Quiz 16—1 Corinthians 11:20
Quiz 17—Luke 8:1–3
Quiz 18—Jeremiah 8:22
Quiz 19—1 Samuel 3:10
Quiz 20—Colossians 4:3
Quiz 21—1 Peter 5:4 initials of words 4 and 5
Quiz 22—Philippians 4:3
Quiz 23—Mark 2:4
Quiz 24—Luke 5:11
Quiz 25—Psalm 98:1
Quiz 26—1 Corinthians 9:8
Quiz 27—Titus 3:13
Quiz 28—Genesis 12:3 starts with second word
Quiz 29—Genesis 35:24
Quiz 30—Matthew 17:3

Look in the Book

Level 9

Quiz 1—Genesis 29:9
Quiz 2—Matthew 10:20
Quiz 3—Psalm 45:9
Quiz 4—Genesis 24:15
Quiz 5—Acts 19:29
Quiz 6—John 9:34
Quiz 7—Hebrews 11:23
Quiz 8—Luke 15:13 first five letters of longest word
Quiz 9—Hebrews 7:19
Quiz 10—Proverbs 20:14
Quiz 11—John 1:46
Quiz 12—Luke 20:39
Quiz 13—Philippians 2:11
Quiz 14—1 Timothy 2:7
Quiz 15—Acts 18:24
Quiz 16—1 Samuel 1:20
Quiz 17—Judges 6:24
Quiz 18—Acts 18:24
Quiz 19—Judges 4:4
Quiz 20—1 Kings 21:7
Quiz 21—Proverbs 17:22
Quiz 22—Genesis 29:12
Quiz 23—Ephesians 5:19
Quiz 24—2 Kings 2:9–10
Quiz 25—Exodus 13:19
Quiz 26—Psalm 116:15
Quiz 27—Matthew 5:14
Quiz 28—Genesis 4:19
Quiz 29—Philippians 4:13
Quiz 30—Acts 10:2 last word

Look in the Book

Level 10

Quiz 1—Proverbs 25:23
Quiz 2—John 11:23
Quiz 3—Luke 14:27
Quiz 4—Luke 1:26
Quiz 5—Acts 8:30
Quiz 6—John 3:7
Quiz 7—Luke 14:2
Quiz 8—Romans 13:8
Quiz 9—Isaiah 43:26
Quiz 10—Job 36:22
Quiz 11—Ezra 7:10
Quiz 12—1 Samuel 16:23
Quiz 13—2 Kings 18:5–6
Quiz 14—Psalm 57:8
Quiz 15—John 4:6
Quiz 16—Hebrews 11:10
Quiz 17—John 4:9; 4:29
Quiz 18—Matthew 11:18
Quiz 19—Isaiah 62:2
Quiz 20—Matthew 28:6
Quiz 21—Matthew 13:53
Quiz 22—1 Timothy 4:13
Quiz 23—Exodus 15:20
Quiz 24—Deuteronomy 19:5
Quiz 25—Genesis 2:14 first five letters begins correct answer
Quiz 26—Acts 1:13–14
Quiz 27—Philippians 2:5
Quiz 28—John 6:63
Quiz 29—Revelation 22:20
Quiz 30—Leviticus 13:29 begins with last word

Look in the Book

Level 11

Quiz 1—Exodus 7:7
Quiz 2—Luke 1:60
Quiz 3—Acts 18:24–26
Quiz 4—Leviticus 27:30
Quiz 5—Job 9:33
Quiz 6—1 Peter 4:16
Quiz 7—Deuteronomy 1:12
Quiz 8—John 11:20
Quiz 9—Hebrews 13:24
Quiz 10—Hebrews 11:5
Quiz 11—Acts 26:30 (similar)
Quiz 12—Ezra 4:18
Quiz 13—Hebrews 11:5
Quiz 14—John 19:20
Quiz 15—1 Corinthians 11:14
Quiz 16—2 Samuel 2:27
Quiz 17—2 Samuel 3:22
Quiz 18—Genesis 17:17
Quiz 19—Proverbs 23:14
Quiz 20—Psalm 65:10 first four letters of word 10
Quiz 21—Amos 7:14
Quiz 22—Ephesians 4:4
Quiz 23—Luke 1:36–37
Quiz 24—Job 26:7
Quiz 25—Matthew 15:14
Quiz 26—Luke 9:62
Quiz 27—Luke 5:20
Quiz 28—Jeremiah 34:10
Quiz 29—Acts 14:12
Quiz 30—Acts 6:11

Look in the Book

Gold

Quiz 1—John 19:39–40
Quiz 2—Ephesians 4:10
Quiz 3—1 Chronicles 26:27
Quiz 4—Isaiah 6:2
Quiz 5—Romans 9:10
Quiz 6—Genesis 25:24
Quiz 7—Genesis 24:22
Quiz 8—Revelation 2:28
Quiz 9—Job 39:26
Quiz 10—John 20:28
Quiz 11—Acts 19:35 third word
Quiz 12—Acts 5:30
Quiz 13—Isaiah 4:6
Quiz 14—John 2:18
Quiz 15—Luke 1:70
Quiz 16—Job 13:18
Quiz 17—John 4:44
Quiz 18—Romans 16:1
Quiz 19—Acts 11:28
Quiz 20—Luke 12:32
Quiz 21—John 18:35 starts with letter of first word
Quiz 22—3 John 1:4
Quiz 23—1 Samuel 1:15
Quiz 24—Galatians 3:9
Quiz 25—John 10:23 begins with letter of last word
Quiz 26—John 16:28
Quiz 27—Romans 12:2
Quiz 28—2 Timothy 1:5
Quiz 29—1 Thessalonians 4:5
Quiz 30—Acts 28:14

Answers

Level 1

Quiz 1—C
Quiz 2—A
Quiz 3—B
Quiz 4—A
Quiz 5—A
Quiz 6—A
Quiz 7—A
Quiz 8—C
Quiz 9—A
Quiz 10—B
Quiz 11—D
Quiz 12—B
Quiz 13—A
Quiz 14—A
Quiz 15—A
Quiz 16—C
Quiz 17—D
Quiz 18—C
Quiz 19—D
Quiz 20—A
Quiz 21—A
Quiz 22—A
Quiz 23—C
Quiz 24—D
Quiz 25—C
Quiz 26—B
Quiz 27—C
Quiz 28—A
Quiz 29—C
Quiz 30—C

Answers

Level 2

Quiz 1—B
Quiz 2—B
Quiz 3—D
Quiz 4—B
Quiz 5—C
Quiz 6—C
Quiz 7—A
Quiz 8—B
Quiz 9—D
Quiz 10—C
Quiz 11—B
Quiz 12—C
Quiz 13—C
Quiz 14—B
Quiz 15—D
Quiz 16—A
Quiz 17—C
Quiz 18—C
Quiz 19—C
Quiz 20—D
Quiz 21—C
Quiz 22—C
Quiz 23—D
Quiz 24—D
Quiz 25—C
Quiz 26—D
Quiz 27—C
Quiz 28—B
Quiz 29—A
Quiz 30—D

Answers

Level 3

Quiz 1—D
Quiz 2—B
Quiz 3—A
Quiz 4—D
Quiz 5—C
Quiz 6—B
Quiz 7—B
Quiz 8—D
Quiz 9—C
Quiz 10—B
Quiz 11—A
Quiz 12—A
Quiz 13—D
Quiz 14—C
Quiz 15—D
Quiz 16—C
Quiz 17—D
Quiz 18—B
Quiz 19—D
Quiz 20—A
Quiz 21—B
Quiz 22—A
Quiz 23—A
Quiz 24—C
Quiz 25—B
Quiz 26—D
Quiz 27—A
Quiz 28—B
Quiz 29—B
Quiz 30—C

Answers

Bronze

Quiz 1—C
Quiz 2—B
Quiz 3—B
Quiz 4—B
Quiz 5—C
Quiz 6—A
Quiz 7—C
Quiz 8—B
Quiz 9—C
Quiz 10—B
Quiz 11—B
Quiz 12—A
Quiz 13—C
Quiz 14—D
Quiz 15—D
Quiz 16—D
Quiz 17—A
Quiz 18—B
Quiz 19—B
Quiz 20—D
Quiz 21—A
Quiz 22—B
Quiz 23—C
Quiz 24—B
Quiz 25—C
Quiz 26—C
Quiz 27—A
Quiz 28—B
Quiz 29—A
Quiz 30—D

Answers

Level 5

Quiz 1—A
Quiz 2—D
Quiz 3—B
Quiz 4—C
Quiz 5—D
Quiz 6—C
Quiz 7—D
Quiz 8—A
Quiz 9—C
Quiz 10—A
Quiz 11—B
Quiz 12—A
Quiz 13—C
Quiz 14—B
Quiz 15—D
Quiz 16—D
Quiz 17—B
Quiz 18—C
Quiz 19—A
Quiz 20—D
Quiz 21—B
Quiz 22—C
Quiz 23—D
Quiz 24—C
Quiz 25—D
Quiz 26—A
Quiz 27—A
Quiz 28—C
Quiz 29—B
Quiz 30—B

Answers

Level 6

Quiz 1—D
Quiz 2—A
Quiz 3—C
Quiz 4—D
Quiz 5—C
Quiz 6—C
Quiz 7—B
Quiz 8—A
Quiz 9—D
Quiz 10—B
Quiz 11—B
Quiz 12—D
Quiz 13—D
Quiz 14—B
Quiz 15—A
Quiz 16—A
Quiz 17—A
Quiz 18—D
Quiz 19—C
Quiz 20—C
Quiz 21—C
Quiz 22—D
Quiz 23—B
Quiz 24—D
Quiz 25—A
Quiz 26—D
Quiz 27—D
Quiz 28—D
Quiz 29—A
Quiz 30—B

Answers

Level 7

Quiz 1—A
Quiz 2—D
Quiz 3—B
Quiz 4—D
Quiz 5—C
Quiz 6—B
Quiz 7—A
Quiz 8—C
Quiz 9—A
Quiz 10—A
Quiz 11—D
Quiz 12—D
Quiz 13—A
Quiz 14—B
Quiz 15—A
Quiz 16—A
Quiz 17—B
Quiz 18—B
Quiz 19—B
Quiz 20—B
Quiz 21—B
Quiz 22—B
Quiz 23—C
Quiz 24—A
Quiz 25—A
Quiz 26—B
Quiz 27—D
Quiz 28—C
Quiz 29—A
Quiz 30—B

Answers

Silver

Quiz 1—A
Quiz 2—B
Quiz 3—A
Quiz 4—C
Quiz 5—A
Quiz 6—D
Quiz 7—B
Quiz 8—A
Quiz 9—B
Quiz 10—C
Quiz 11—B
Quiz 12—C
Quiz 13—D
Quiz 14—C
Quiz 15—C
Quiz 16—B
Quiz 17—C
Quiz 18—C
Quiz 19—D
Quiz 20—B
Quiz 21—D
Quiz 22—B
Quiz 23—A
Quiz 24—A
Quiz 25—D
Quiz 26—C
Quiz 27—A
Quiz 28—A
Quiz 29—B
Quiz 30—D

Answers

Level 9

Quiz 1—A
Quiz 2—D
Quiz 3—B
Quiz 4—C
Quiz 5—C
Quiz 6—D
Quiz 7—A
Quiz 8—A
Quiz 9—B
Quiz 10—D
Quiz 11—B
Quiz 12—A
Quiz 13—D
Quiz 14—D
Quiz 15—B
Quiz 16—D
Quiz 17—B
Quiz 18—C
Quiz 19—B
Quiz 20—B
Quiz 21—B
Quiz 22—D
Quiz 23—D
Quiz 24—C
Quiz 25—B
Quiz 26—A
Quiz 27—C
Quiz 28—B
Quiz 29—C
Quiz 30—B

Answers

Level 10

Quiz 1—A
Quiz 2—A
Quiz 3—A
Quiz 4—B
Quiz 5—A
Quiz 6—C
Quiz 7—D
Quiz 8—A
Quiz 9—B
Quiz 10—B
Quiz 11—A
Quiz 12—C
Quiz 13—B
Quiz 14—B
Quiz 15—D
Quiz 16—D
Quiz 17—C
Quiz 18—B
Quiz 19—A
Quiz 20—A
Quiz 21—A
Quiz 22—B
Quiz 23—D
Quiz 24—B
Quiz 25—B
Quiz 26—D
Quiz 27—A
Quiz 28—D
Quiz 29—A
Quiz 30—B

Answers

Level 11

Quiz 1—A
Quiz 2—B
Quiz 3—D
Quiz 4—D
Quiz 5—B
Quiz 6—B
Quiz 7—D
Quiz 8—C
Quiz 9—D
Quiz 10—A
Quiz 11—D
Quiz 12—B
Quiz 13—B
Quiz 14—C
Quiz 15—A
Quiz 16—C
Quiz 17—C
Quiz 18—D
Quiz 19—B
Quiz 20—B
Quiz 21—D
Quiz 22—D
Quiz 23—D
Quiz 24—B
Quiz 25—B
Quiz 26—A
Quiz 27—C
Quiz 28—B
Quiz 29—B
Quiz 30—B

Answers

Gold

Quiz 1—A
Quiz 2—B
Quiz 3—A
Quiz 4—D
Quiz 5—B
Quiz 6—B
Quiz 7—A
Quiz 8—C
Quiz 9—C
Quiz 10—B
Quiz 11—A
Quiz 12—B
Quiz 13—D
Quiz 14—C
Quiz 15—B
Quiz 16—B
Quiz 17—A
Quiz 18—B
Quiz 19—D
Quiz 20—B
Quiz 21—D
Quiz 22—D
Quiz 23—C
Quiz 24—D
Quiz 25—D
Quiz 26—A
Quiz 27—D
Quiz 28—A
Quiz 29—C
Quiz 30—D